It's Gotta

The John Von Ohlen Story

Jim Nunn

ISBN: 978-1-944581-06-0

Shadow Books
Cincinnati, Ohio

Printed in the United States of America

10 9 8 7 6 5 4

For Jeff Hamilton

"A great friend and the greatest drummer."

- John Von Ohlen

Acknowledgements

Cover Photo: John Zappa

Photographs: Kauai's Hindu Monastery, Joe Gaudio, and Don Foley

Roebling Point Coffee & Books

Cincinnati Public Library

Editorial: Allison Haden

To provide comments, feedback, or inquire about bulk quantity discounts, contact:

Jim Nunn: jimnunn57@gmail.com

It's Gotta Swing:
The John Von Ohlen Story

The Music Begins

The hi-hat cymbals whispered as the air swept through the two open silver plates, followed by a confident downbeat on the snare. The drummer moved into a swinging tempo on the ride and the band was in full motion. Folks were pouring into the joint, including a young man following the sounds like a dog making a beeline toward a bone. This was the beginning, but only the beginning.

The music of the big-band thunderclap was a warm-up act for a lifelong love affair. Like so many things in life, the loudest of messages can happen when we least expect them. And like so many stories, it starts with a pretty girl. You can't beat a pretty pair of legs, especially to a fourteen-year-old boy. That's what drew John to Charlotte all those years ago. "It was her legs—she had great legs," Von Ohlen reminisces with a smile. This was the first time John had ever gone on a date. It was also the night that he got hooked on the drums. From that night forward he says, "I was a drummer," even though he hadn't played a lick and didn't sit down behind a drum set until much later.

It was 1955, and the Stan Kenton Orchestra was playing at Westlake Ballroom in Indianapolis. The band had traveled down from Chicago after recently recording the popular album *Contemporary Concepts*. The Orchestra was hot. Ray Von Ohlen, John's father, volunteered to drive the young couple to the show. Charlotte, Ray, and John were walking from the parking lot toward what turned out to be a packed house of over five hundred fans. And John still remembers the sound of Mel Lewis working his cymbal as they crossed the parking lot. To this day, he can tell you that it was a twenty-inch medium heavy ping cymbal. Once inside, they could see the place was hopping with people already swinging to the music. There were a few tables in back but because it was a dance hall, sitting was not a priority. John volunteered to scout up front while his date and his father grabbed seats in back.

The future drummer followed the hypnotizing sound of Lewis on that cymbal like a mouse following a trail of cheese crumbs until he was standing right in front of the drummer. The rest is history; John was never the same. From the catbird seat directly in front of Lewis he stood, with the crowd pressed up against the stage. Mesmerized, he watched in awe. At intermission he thought of going back to look for his companions, but he knew the crowd would swallow his position up front.

Kenton always carried a band of close to two-dozen musicians to create the orchestral sound he was known for, and that night was no exception. The players were arranged on a two-foot-high stage. John was hypnotized—he couldn't take his eyes off the drummer! The place was swinging and those lucky enough to be up front were carried away by the blast of music from the full band coming together. Mel Lewis had a distinct sound on the drums, especially his unique style of playing the cymbals. He added a quality to the Stan Kenton sound that was impossible to emulate. Even the great Buddy Rich once said, "Mel Lewis doesn't sound like anybody except himself." When you watch John play even now you see uniqueness in how he works and solos on the cymbals, perhaps a reflection of his affinity for Lewis. Getting the sound on ride cymbals sets the swinging rhythm for everything that follows. Mel locked in with snare and bass drum, throwing in fills on the toms, always including a variety of sounds in working the hi-hat, ride, and crash cymbals.

Charlotte and John never went on a second date, and he felt bad about deserting her and his father in back, but his heart was already spoken for. After that night, after that moment, John will tell you his life was changed forever: "The next day when I woke up I was a drummer." He may not have owned a drum set or had the money to get one, but all obstacles would eventually be overcome. In his mind, he was a drummer.

Some musicians start on the drums and gravitate to other instruments. Not Von Ohlen. He'd studied the trombone and the piano for close to ten years. This served as a strong foundation in reading and understanding music. But watching and listening to Mel Lewis that night was like being hit in the face. Using his own words, he was "transformed."

This book is a rim shot. In drumming, a rim shot is not a subtle stroke. It's an attention getter. A quick and accentuating sound that leaps off the snare. Consider this book a rim shot to grab your attention. John Von Ohlen's life journey deserves to be told, so we've pulled together some of the parts and pieces that are essential to the person he is now.

John was born in Indianapolis, Indiana, on May 13, 1941. John's parents separated soon after he was born, leaving him to be raised by his father, Ray, and his grandmother, Bertha. Bertha lived with John and Ray until John was well into his teens. The grandmother had a strong, "take no prisoners" belief about the importance of religion and the evils of music, girls, and many of life's pleasures.

She would yell and preach about sin, including music and jazz. The two had hell-raising arguments, but fortunately when it just didn't seem that they could coexist under the same roof any longer, Ray was ready to remarry. It was time for Bertha to find other living arrangements. She played a big role in raising John until he was sixteen. It took him a long time to silence the angry lectures and beliefs that echoed in his mind after she was gone.

John's father was a loving and positive source of support for the future drummer. Ray worked as a route delivery man for a potato chip company. Money was tight, but he did all he could to provide for John. Although he didn't play himself, Ray had a good ear for music. He introduced his son to music at four or five years old, passing on 78s that went from Count Basie to classical.

Photos: 1. A very young John Von Ohlen. 2. Age six or seven with his father Ray in downtown Indianapolis.

12

Ray supported John's interests in local sports too. It wasn't unusual for father and son to wander down to the local ball field for a round of pitch and catch. Ray was an avid reader, billiard player, and competitive chess player. When his father passed away, John learned more about how dedicated his father was in the city to working with disadvantaged youth, especially the local Boy's Clubs. Ray was an interesting, good-hearted man, and a positive influence on John. He purchased his son a used accordion before John was five years old. Not long after, John started in on piano lessons and continued for almost ten years.

Thanks to the support from his father, he got a trombone

CHOOL DAYS 1954-55
SCHOOL NO 58

when he was ten years old, and not long after started playing in the school band. Over time the youngster even started playing professionally. John enjoyed it all and with just a bit of encouragement can still kick out an impressive riff or two on the piano.

It would be three more years after hearing Mel Lewis and the Stan Kenton Orchestra before John got the chance to sit behind a drum set on any kind of regular basis. The opportunity came when a neighbor, Dick Norris, acquired a new set of Gretsch drums. The timing couldn't have been better for John, or worse for Dick. No sooner had he purchased the set than he was notified by the United States Navy to report for active duty. For a twelve-dollar monthly rental fee, John finally had his drum set. Norris still owns that same set to this day.

Photo: John at age thirteen.

Gretsch is a well-respected maker of musical instruments, and the drum set was top-notch. Suddenly John had an

entire set including snare, bass, toms, and cymbals. He quickly moved his father's Admiral Hi-Fi into his bedroom and played, and played, and played. By day he used drumsticks to accompany Big Bands at full volume on the record player. At night John would switch to the softer sound of brushes. The drum set and Admiral phonograph left little room for anything besides the bed in his bedroom. He lived and breathed music. When the household went to sleep, John would lie in bed staring at the set.

The family lived in the city, and by odd coincidence—or maybe it was just another piece of John's inevitable destiny—there was a school for the deaf not far from their house. For a young man obsessed with drumming, it could only be considered an omen that the next-door neighbors were deaf. John could drum away from dawn to dusk with little concern about complaints of loud sounds emanating from the Von Ohlen house.

As John drummed, he worked to make sense of the rhythms and beats coming from the record player. He benefited tremendously from ten years of piano lessons and five on the trombone. He mixed these experiences with his natural talents, and played. Later in life John would be confronted with the need to learn basic drumming rudiments: paradiddles, rolls, and the calisthenics that are required of all well-rounded professional drummers.

Photo: Von Ohlen's senior picture.

But within the confines of the four walls of his bedroom, John taught himself how to play jazz and swing. He was developing the very early style points that would make for the unique sound of John Von Ohlen the drummer.

For months, John played along with records by Count Basie, Duke Ellington, Stan Kenton, and a collection of musicians from the growing West Coast jazz scene. Finding the determination to play the drums hour after hour wasn't an issue; heck, drumming was now the heart and soul of John's life. And it showed. He remembers his dad telling him one night at the dinner table that something was happening. Something was changing in how John played the drums. At first Ray said it was just noise, but now there was a rhythm—a beat. The sounds that poured down from John's upstairs bedroom were "making sense," Ray said. Starting with that mesmerizing experience of watching Mel Lewis, John had leaped forward on a musical journey that is still going on sixty years later.

Of course, once John had secured the Gretsch drum set, his next move was rearranging his schedule to accommodate priorities. He wanted more practice time. The first thing to go was high school—unbeknownst to his father.

Photo: Senior year at North Central High School.

As neighborhoods and enrollments grew, so did the need for more schools. John was enrolled at Short Ridge High for his freshman and sophomore years, and then the family moved. He then spent three years (yes, three) at North Central High. John was now driving himself to North Central. In the early morning his father and stepmother would leave for work. John went off in the direction of North Central only to circle back home, back to his room, and the drums.

Von Ohlen had to repeat his senior year because he consistently skipped school. By that time he was also good enough to land a weekend gig around town playing drums with a local talent named the Don Foley Orchestra.

Photo: John at the drums playing with the Don Foley Orchestra on weekends while he and Don were still in high school. This was one of his first paying gigs.

In 1960, John got his diploma and left home for the new world of the University of North Texas. Located an hour from Dallas in Denton, Texas, UNT is home to one of the premier music programs in the country. In 1947 it became the first university in the world to offer a degree in jazz studies. Alumni include Herb Ellis, Grammy Award-winning musician Bob Belden, and Jimmy Giuffre, who played with and composed for Woody Herman. Stan Kenton, Herman, and others regularly pulled their supporting cast from the musical training ground in Denton.

Texas and the Dallas area were rich with playing opportunities, and before long John wandered from the classroom to play live gigs full-time with local musicians. He was twenty. Today, he laments that young students spend so much time in the classroom with little time or emphasis devoted to working gigs with various bands. At the time, the area was teeming with opportunity and music. And what better way to learn than playing on a regular basis with seasoned professionals?

Ralph Marterie

Before long, John caught on with Ralph Marterie and his fourteen-piece orchestra. Ralph wasn't a pure jazzman and didn't pretend to be. He had a touring dance band. One of his talents as a band man was recognizing and playing whatever the masses wanted to hear. This was just the kind of training ground John thrived in as he developed his chops and talents to play whatever the music demanded.

In addition to the diversity of music, the young and curious Von Ohlen thrived on the freedom and late hours. Another byproduct of playing the clubs was that the late-night scene attracted plenty of opportunities to get to know the opposite sex, and to enjoy drink and drugs.

Ralph Marterie and His Orchestra crisscrossed the country playing a wide variety of venues. For nearly two years John and the group lived the grind of highways, back roads, and long bus rides. It was a great training ground musically, and a non-stop traveling party fueled by booze and pills.

Von Ohlen was twenty years old and doing what he wanted to do, which was play music. He was building a solid foundation in the business. He was meeting other musicians and making friendships that would last for decades, like his friendship with trumpeter Jerry Conrad, who John played with on a variety of gigs—including John's years with Rosemary Clooney.

The devil is in the details, and for John the details were bad news. He became seriously hooked on amphetamines. He could get anything he wanted from the guys in the back of the bus and he developed contacts elsewhere. Drugs were everywhere. John would go on binges that would sometimes last a week or more. That meant literally not sleeping for seven to ten days. It was crazy and John knew it. If he didn't somehow quit, this was going to kill him.

His efforts to stop were futile; he'd give up the pills for weeks at a time, but then crash big time. He'd feel miserable, depressed with all sorts of dark and nagging thoughts. So he'd go on another bender.

Marterie put up with John's reckless behavior because the music worked. The band sounded tight and was successful, with plenty of gigs throughout the country. But looking back it's a time of blurred dark memories for John.

While playing with Ralph Marterie and His Orchestra, John was contacted by two outfits that would play a big role in his future. In 1963, Stan Kenton needed a drummer and approached him about joining Kenton's band, and John jumped. With little thought, Von Ohlen told Ralph he appreciated all that Ralph had done for him, but he was moving on. At the last minute Kenton changed his mind and decided to use his horn player Dee Barton, who was also a talented drummer and knew Kenton's catalog of tunes. Today John says this was a blessing in disguise because he wasn't ready for the challenge of backing the Stan Kenton Orchestra musically or emotionally.

The second call came in the fall of 1963 and left little choice as to what John's next step would be. The United States government had a job for John Von Ohlen. He'd been drafted.

A New Training Ground: The United States Army

The war in Vietnam had not yet reached the level of American military involvement that it would later in the 1960s. However, the United States had close to sixteen thousand troops and advisers stationed in the country by the end of 1963. President Kennedy was in office and the US military was still attempting to operate primarily in an advisory capacity, resulting in limited direct military engagement. As anyone who lived through that era or reads the history books can attest, with each passing month our involvement and casualties increased.

Like many Americans, John had no strong feeling about the politics that were just beginning to unfold in Southeast Asia, but the military had not been a part of the young musician's career plans. Thus, he was not excited by the sudden change his life would be taking, but had little choice in the matter. Von Ohlen reported to the base at Fort Knox for Basic Training. During John's eight-week stint he was trained to fight in the infantry.

A possible alternative to carrying a gun through the rice paddies of Vietnam came via a friend and mentor by the name of Jim Edison. Edison was adamant in instructing John that he should audition for the military marching band. John laughs as he remembers the terror the troop sergeant struck in the hearts of many a young recruit, including John. But as Jim pointed out, army rules dictated that anyone who wanted to apply for the marching band could do so. Four weeks into his stint, John got up the courage and approached the sergeant.

Ray Stracci was the drummer on base in charge of auditions. Prior to entering the army, Stracci had also played professionally. Priority number one for a drummer in the Military Marching Band is snare work. Beyond that it can be a bass drum or even cymbals. Any drummer can tell you that the fundamentals of drumming focus on what are called the "rudiments." And mastering the rudiments of stick control was very important in the kind of drumming required in the military and marching bands.

The birthplace of rudimental drumming is thought to be France back in the 1800s. Drummers in the King's Honor Guard were expected to learn thirteen specific sticking strokes. The number of rudiments listed as the fundamentals of drumming by people who care about that kind of thing today is sometimes said to be twenty-six or more. But these thirteen fundamentals or rudiments of drumming make up the foundation and include single-stroke drum rolls, double strokes, diddles, paradiddles (two single strokes followed by a double stroke), and so on.

At this stage in John's musical life he was self-taught when it came to drumming. During those early months of drumming in his bedroom he didn't even know what the hi-hat was used for. Then came the advanced training he received courtesy of dance halls and gin joints with Ralph Marterie. He knew how to support and lead a band on a drum set as evidenced by his successes, and he was getting very good at it. But when it came to mastering or understanding the fundamentals of drumming as taught in the classroom, he got a failing grade. Specific drum strokes such as flams and drags were not a part of his musical vocabulary or his skill set.

The audition did not go well. In fact, it was a disaster. John's playing was terrible and it looked like he was destined to spend his time developing skills with a rifle instead of a snare drum. But Von Ohlen explained to Stracci that he had traveled and played with Ralph Marterie for almost two years. They'd cut three albums. John explained that his background was playing on a whole set, swinging with the toms, snare, cymbals, and floor bass. Ray knew of Ralph Marterie and His Orchestra, and he figured anyone who could keep up with the band had the chops. John promised Ray that over the thirteen weeks of practice time members received prior to actually performing, he would master the rudiments required to play with a marching band. Ray took a chance on him and John was in. To this day Von Ohlen is indebted to Ray Stracci for the confidence Stracci showed in him, and for possibly saving his life.

In many ways, life continued as it had prior to being drafted once John was in as a drummer with the military band at Fort Knox. By day he was a member of the United States Army marching band. By night John looked for any gig he could find, which generally meant rock 'n' roll. Along with the late hours and gigs, he gravitated right back to pills and booze. There was no stopping the headfirst backslide into what he had been doing the last couple of years. He was a mess, going on binges and keeping insane hours. Often little more was required in his day job than to make morning roll call, and sometimes that was a challenge. It was the '60s, and John was immersed in the music scene, bars, and nightlife. At one point he even wandered all the way back home to Indianapolis for over a week, not even thinking about the consequences. In the military, AWOL is a serious infraction.

Photo: Von Ohlen, just after Boot Camp—1961.

Fortunately, because of the more lax standards for members of the military band compared to other soldiers, his sergeant let him off the hook. Von Ohlen explained his absence was due to an illness in the family. The sergeant just shook his head in disbelief. Nothing else came of it and he was not court marshaled.

As time dragged on, John knew something had to give. His behavior was out of control. He knew these ten-day, amphetamine-fueled binges were going to kill him. When he was in Indianapolis he even had a pharmacist friend who would load him up with all the speed he wanted. He had the wisdom to know he couldn't and didn't want to go on like this, to die like this. His first desperate step was to get away from the routine that was enabling his current lifestyle.

John heard about an opening for a drummer to play with a military touring band called Show Mobile. The group was based out of Fort Meade in Maryland. Prior to the army, John had cut a record for Decca with a group called the College All-Stars. The music was good; it even included a sixteen-year-old Keith Jarrett playing on his first-ever recording. John knew that getting out of town would provide a big first step. He needed a change of scenery away from his pals and the familiar temptations around Fort Knox. He applied for the gig and sent along a copy of the All-Stars record.

John was accepted into Show Mobile and transferred to the East Coast. Landing the gig was the easy part in creating change. Von Ohlen flew to Maryland on a military plane at the very end of 1964 and immediately attempted to climb on the wagon and go clean. No booze and certainly no pills. Cigarettes were it.

John can still remember cold January mornings as he sat on the bed in his barracks telling himself, "just today." To stay sober for just that one day. His goal was "one day at a time." He was unfamiliar with that same AA creed that is one of the core principles of the organization. Making it through the dark thoughts and staying sober for twenty-four hours was all he could hope for. Tomorrow anything could happen, he just had to make it through today clean. John kept it together but was miserable, depressed, and searching for any meaning to life that could help him get out of this self-imposed hell. It was that bad. His body was going through withdrawal while he danced with his demons.

John felt blessed by the love from his father. But there were other loud voices echoing around his head. He heard the strict angry screaming of his grandmother lecturing about temptation and sin. He tried to come to terms with his mother leaving to start another life so soon after he was born.

Music and the drums had provided a sanctuary but that safe-haven had only lasted so long. Then it was two years of life on the road where anything goes as long as he could play the gig, followed by the army and Fort Knox. Life had been a train wreck on pills and now all the demons he'd been dancing with were back louder and crazier than ever.

Many people look back and see individuals and events that are turning points in life. This is certainly the case for John. One of his bandmates in Show Mobile was a pianist named Ed Zimmerman. Zimmerman overheard John say he'd been reading about Swami Vivekananda. Vivekananda was an Indian Hindu monk. In the 1800s Swami introduced Indian philosophies to the Western world, raising interfaith awareness and bringing Hinduism to the status of a major world religion during the late-nineteenth century.

When Ed learned of John's spiritual interest and searching, they began to talk. The two spent hours together. John was confused and in pain. Zimmerman seemed to know all the right questions to ask and was a great listener who didn't pass judgment. In their discussions, he drew on beliefs associated with Hinduism and the teachings of the important teachers, like Swami Vivekananda. Ed Zimmerman helped open another door for the young Von Ohlen.

Ed talked about his own spiritual leader, Sivaya Subramuniyaswami, who would later simply be known as "Master." Born in Oakland in 1927, Subramuniyaswami dedicated his entire life to spiritual enlightenment. He traveled to Sri Lanka and India in 1949 meditating, practicing yoga, and studying Hinduism and other forms of spiritual teaching. In 1957 he founded what is now Himalayan Academy and opened America's first Hindu temple near Presidio Park in Northern California.

The World Religious Parliament in New Delhi would one day actually honor Master (Sivaya Subramuniyaswami) as one of five modern-day "Jagadacharyas"—or international religious teachers—who had most dynamically promoted Hinduism in the past twenty-five years.

With the help of Ed Zimmerman, John was discovering something in addition to music that made sense and drew his energies. His creative and curious spirit wanted more. He researched and read literature that continued to speak to the deeper questions he carried.

Ed was a devoted follower and would speak with Master every week by phone. Before long, John spoke with Master too. During these conversations, more started to come together and they clicked. This was the beginning of a much deeper relationship that shaped the rest of John's life. Later John would show his father literature explaining some of the teachings and his dad responded, "I knew I'd never have to worry about you again."

While still stationed at Fort Mead John used a two-week pass to travel with Ed on a military B-52 to San Francisco. The two then proceeded on to Sivaya's ashram. It wasn't until he actually met him that John realized he was a holy man. His more intense studies with the monks and Sivaya (Master) had begun. With such a deeply spiritual and personal journey, it is hard for John to put into simple words how his beliefs and worldview were changing.

Back to Music

John was tapping into a new energy for life. His musical skills continued to develop too. He started to communicate with friends and mentors like Mel Lewis. The first time they talked, John boldly picked up the phone and contacted the famous drummer with ten questions he'd collected about drumming. John doesn't remember what the questions were, but he does remember that Mel couldn't have been kinder as he took the call from his home in New York and talked with Von Ohlen. John's world was expanding. He was looking for answers outside of music as well. Still just a young man, he was beginning to look at the universe in ways that would be reflected in every aspect of his life.

In 1965, John completed his tour with the United States Army. He traveled to New York City to enjoy his new freedom and explore the music scene. "Catting around," as John called it. One of the first clubs he visited had a guy on the drums who was terrific. The drummer was using brushes as he worked the snare, hi-hat, and ride cymbal. Man, could this guy swing, and he made everybody on stage better. For those unfamiliar with music and playing the drums, playing with brushes is a separate skill from using wooden sticks. John immediately told himself, "I can't move here, there is so much talent already." It was only later that he discovered the drummer was Jake Hanna, considered one of the best. The two drummers became good friends and began hanging out together. Jake could play anything, and played with the biggest names in show business. Woody Herman's orchestra was good, but when Hanna was his drummer for three years they were sensational. Jake was the house drummer on the *Merv Griffin Show* for years. John would accompany him and often sit right underneath a cymbal, off camera absorbing all he could.

Within a few months, John left New York City and returned to Indiana. He landed a gig with the three-piece house band at The Embers nightclub. The Embers was a popular supper club in Indianapolis throughout the '60s. The entire city has been a launching pad for talent, and in those days it was an important stopover to some of the biggest names in jazz, including Charlie Parker, Miles Davis, Wes Montgomery, and Max Roach.

The country was a different entertainment scene in the mid-1960s. There were more nightclubs, with a cast of talent on the road traveling to these different venues. Rodney Dangerfield might be in town for a few nights, followed by another comedian or entertainer. Most of the acts couldn't afford to have their own troupe of traveling musicians backing them from show to show. The house band at Embers and elsewhere might be made up by a thirty-piece orchestra to support these road shows. In today's entertainment landscape, the nightclub scene has dwindled primarily to New York City and a handful of cities like Chicago. To cut costs, the clubs that do remain often use a couple of house musicians or recorded music.

One of the bands that played Indianapolis regularly was Billy Maxted and His Manhattan Jazz Band. Once John heard them he wanted to be a part of Maxted's seven-piece traveling troupe. As fate would have it, Maxted felt the same way about John. He'd heard him play a few times and wanted him as his drummer. Thus came young Von Ohlen's first big-name opportunity. He'd played with plenty of quality musicians, but this was a step up. Billy played piano and wrote music. This included arrangements for Benny Goodman, Will Bradley, and Claude Thornhill. His composition "Manhattan Spiritual" was a top-ten hit for Reggie Owen in 1959. Probably the biggest hit for the Manhattan Jazz Band was a swing version of "Satin Doll" in 1961.

Playing with the Manhattan Jazz Band was a good gig for John. The band operated on all cylinders, and John had the chance to further develop and demonstrate his skills. Maxted had called Long Island home for years and played regularly at a joint called Nick's, in Greenwich Village. He eventually migrated south to Florida, and with John on drums the band landed a long-standing gig at the Florida Beach Club Hotel in Ft. Lauderdale. Maxted's band never hit the big leagues, but they had a strong and loyal following.

There are certain expected licks that a drummer playing with a jazz band has to be on top of for the scripted musical notes. He is the timekeeper for the entire band. But there is also room for improvising, and John's formal training gave him room to be creative and really swing in between the beats the band counted on him to keep.

It was 1967. After less than two years with Maxted, an offer came from Woody Herman's manager to join Herman's Thundering Herd. For John, this was not an easy decision. Moving on with Woody was an opportunity to step up his game even further and be a part of one of the most well-known orchestras in the country. But staying put with Billy had its appeal too, and he initially planned to turn down the offer. John valued what he had with Maxted's band. Not only was it a regular gig, the band was hot. Billy knew how to get the most out of his band, with parts written to highlight individual players' skills, like the talented Von Ohlen on drums. Billy Maxted and His Manhattan Jazz Band had just recorded an album and in their smaller world they were operating on all four cylinders.

At a musical crossroads, John turned to someone for guidance who would play an increasingly important role in his life: Sivaya Subramuniyaswami. Master counseled John to listen to his inner voices and desires. He told John that "name and fame" was what he wanted in life. Show business is a funny animal; it is unlike other businesses because it is so deeply rooted in emotion. That music was not always just about artistic creativity; this was the entertainment industry. Ego and emotions were often greater influencers for people in show business than other endeavors, and at this early stage in John's career that was true.

As they talked further, Von Ohlen realized what Master was saying was true. He'd always wanted to be on the road with a top-notch band, a great one. Woody Herman was one of the biggest names around, and at this point in his life John wanted the whole package. He wanted name and fame and a chance to play with one of the hottest bands on the national scene. He made the decision and phoned Woody Herman's manager.

Master had predicted that Maxted would throw all sorts of reasons in John's face as to why John just couldn't leave. And he did. Maxted told John that he'd created a great band and John was a big part of it, featured on the drums. Master even predicted that Billy would threaten to quit the business, to give it all up. Sure enough, he did—threaten, that is.

This wasn't the first time John would be faced with tough decisions about his musical journey. He felt an obligation to Billy Maxted and His Manhattan Jazz Band and the guys connected with it. But this was a calling he couldn't deny. His skills had opened a door for him and he was going to walk through it. John stood by his decision and over the next two weeks, he and Maxted mended fences and parted on good terms, with Billy giving John his blessings. Reminiscing years later, Von Ohlen smiles as he says that Maxted later told him he found an even better drummer to replace John. When John heard his replacement play, he had to agree the new guy was good.

John packed his drums and moved on to play with Woody Herman and the New Thundering Herd, sometimes also referred to as the Young Thundering Herd back then. This was a chance for Von Ohlen to step into the top tier of big-band entertainment. One thing it didn't mean was job security. Woody was known to go through drummers right and left. Just a few days before joining the New Herd, John found himself not far from Indianapolis in Cincinnati, the same town that Woody's band was playing in. Without announcing his presence he sat in the back of the club listening to the band, and they sounded good. Looking back John says the drummer was good too, but possibly better suited to trios and smaller bands. Maybe he just didn't know how to handle the power of a Big Band.

As he sat in the shadows nursing a beer, John didn't want Woody to discover he was there. He was worried the bandleader would ask him to sit in, and after a listen perhaps decide he didn't dig John's chops after all. Darn if the trumpet player (who was also the manager) didn't notice John and introduce him to Woody Herman, who immediately said, "Hey, why don't you sit in?" The Herd's future drummer replied, "No man, I gotta get back to Indianapolis."

Woody Herman

In the first days with the New Thundering Herd things were good. John believed he was finding his place musically with the band and they were swinging. But things quickly took a downward turn. In music, the bass and drums are keepers of the clock. They are the timekeepers, and it is imperative that they are in sync. In the beginning, John and the bass player found that solid groove together. Woody's original bassist and John sounded good and spoke the same musical language. But after only a week he moved on and a new bassist came on board.

John and Carl Pruett never could find that tight sound together. It was nothing about not getting along with Carl. Looking back on it, Von Ohlen understands they just never found the space to anticipate and complement each other's sound. It was a musical thing that made for a less-than-top-notch swinging sound in John's opinion. He probably shouldn't put it all on Carl; maybe John lacked the self-confidence to take control. He tried to relax but struggled to get the time or the right groove. The other musicians heard it too, and would bark at John. Carl was a "thumper" on the bass, and John says he "just couldn't get anything off him, and it all depends on the bass, not the drums."

Woody never mentioned any concerns, which added to John's frustrations. He told Von Ohlen he liked the way the drums were sounding. For John, the days with Woody were a travel log of sites and an introduction into the entertainment industry on a whole new level. The Herd with John on drums traveled the entire country and Europe, playing with some of the biggest names in music.

They headlined the *Ed Sullivan Show* along with Tony Bennett and Shirley Bassey. The band performed with Bennett and played their hit tune "Woody's Boogaloo."

They later toured with Tony for a couple of weeks in 1967. They used big-band charts written by Torrie Zito and the band would just catch fire. After the first show of the tour, Tony walked back through the curtain and reached out to John to shake his hand; "Man, I could feel you the whole way—it was great." John always kept a monitor in front of him so he could be sure to hear the singer. Not long after, Bennett moved on to playing trios and the two didn't cross paths much after that.

Herman's band backed Frankie Laine. Often called "America's number-one song stylist" and nicknamed "Mr. Steel Tonsils" for how versatile he was, it was always fun and John enjoyed playing with him. He sang an eclectic variety of song styles and genres, stretching from big band to pop. Laine sang some of the more well-known theme songs for Western soundtracks, such as *Rawhide*. There's a special talent in playing with singers, and so many like Laine appreciated the skill John had in backing them.

John had hit the big time in playing with Herman's New Thundering Herd. He was in the major leagues and he continued to develop his skills. Woody was good to John and taught him a lot about the business, but John was growing restless and unsatisfied. He suspects years later that he could have voiced his frustrations to Woody, and Herman might have found another bass player, but it never crossed John's mind.

John had planned to ride with the Herd awhile longer. If you played with Woody Herman for two years you could write your own ticket, getting studio work, working with other bands, whatever you wanted. But after a year John quit the band. He was unhappy with the music and even angry that Woody didn't hear it, or maybe he did and just chose not to do anything. Von Ohlen liked Carl, who was an entertainer or a bit of a "showboat" on stage. They'd have good nights every now and then, but they were few and far between. The music just wasn't working for John. Looking back he remembers talking to the great jazz drummer Don Lamond, who had played with Woody. Don told him exactly what would happen, "You won't play well or sound great but you'll have a few terrific nights that'll keep you going."

When John explained to Woody that he was leaving, the bandmaster took it in his usual calm fashion. John told Woody he had a trip to the Alps planned, and that he was going to go on a kind of spiritual sabbatical. Woody tried to convince John to stay, but after a few minutes slowly stood up, said "peace," and walked away. Woody Herman had seen it all. He later told *Down Beat* magazine, "Yea, we train 'em and they leave." At the time John was still frustrated by Woody, frustrated that the leader didn't do anything. But as he looks back his memories have softened a bit. Woody taught John a lot about the entertainment business and about music. "Woody never said a whole lot, but he had this way of looking at you and you knew. Sometimes I would drop into the beat and just get that feeling, and Woody would turn around and smile. Woody taught me a lot."

California and Beyond

After talking to Woody and giving him a couple more weeks, John traveled to Northern California and settled in San Francisco. He knew he wanted to be closer to the ashram and Master, but beyond that he wasn't sure what he might do next. Master suggested it would be good for John to try other things, other experiences. He was at a crossroads with music. He didn't look for any kind of regular gig. Von Ohlen picked up a few odd jobs to pay the bills and eventually landed work in an upscale restaurant. Weeks started to turn into months. One day John visited the manager of the restaurant to tell him he'd decided he wanted to start working as a waiter. The manager said, "OK," and they discussed what was next.

It was late afternoon as John walked out of the meeting, working his way from the back of the restaurant past dining tables toward the lounge area. Into the bar walked a young guy carrying pieces of a drum set. He was part of the night's entertainment and he had his hands full juggling cymbals and drums. Suddenly it was like John had been hit by a bolt of lightning, what he called "an epiphany."

"Man, I am a drummer—that's it" John thought. He quit the restaurant job that same day and started playing music. Any kind of gig, he just wanted to get behind the drums again and start making music.

Before long, life took another dramatic turn. John visited Master at the chapel, which also served as the ashram. Master was still working with young people locally and following more of a Christian path. He was very dedicated to yoga and alternative spiritual paths, but was still known locally as "Father."

Over time he would move completely away from Christian beliefs. Master, or "Father," was planning a world tour that would start in Paris and quickly move on to Tibet and India, including Mumbai and the Himalayas.

John decided the tour was not for him. He was visiting the ashram with regularity but was also focused on finding work and living day-to-day. Then Von Ohlen walked by a wall poster that stopped him in his tracks. It was a large photograph of a beautiful valley leading up to the spectacular Himalaya mountain range, home to the world's highest mountains.

John had visited his fill of jazz joints. He'd sat in the back of buses traveling thousands of miles to small towns and big cities across the United States. He had never seen, let alone visited, anywhere as breathtaking as what he saw on that poster.

Photo: Master at top center of photo with arms spread wide. John is located lower right center.

So it wasn't some overpowering yearning for greater spiritual awareness that drew him. It was the beauty of what he saw in the photos. That's what convinced Von Ohlen to take out a loan so he could travel on the world tour.

This would prove to be the first of two trips to India with Master. It was 1969 when John left music behind, focusing on hours of yoga, meditation, and exploring different religious teachings. Along with Master, the monks, and other followers the tour totaled close to sixty people. They traveled to countries in Europe, Russia, Japan, and high into the Himalayas, Burma, and Siam.

Mumbai, known as Bombay until 1995, is the most populated city in India, currently with over eighteen million citizens. The day they arrived, there was a dense, wet, early-morning fog slowly lifting as the bus drove across a long bridge into Mumbai all those years ago. As the mist cleared, John could see a flatbed truck up ahead. The truck would stop, and a worker would jump down from the side and lift dead bodies that had collected along the roadway. John had never before seen anything like what he was witnessing. How many westerners have? Dharavi, an area in Mumbai, has one of the largest slums in the world, with a population of close to one million. The poverty and economics in India have improved in the last fifty years, but the country still has some of the worst poverty, along with some of the greatest wealth in the world.

India had one of the largest populations of people infected with leprosy. The country has become much more health-aware, including working to eradicate the disease since the late 1960s when John first visited. As Master's tour group continued to travel in Mumbai, they walked through a leper colony.

To this day the experience is with John. The tragedy and terrible sadness he felt being around people who were treated as total outcasts was overwhelming. His group walked among hundreds of crying, pleading, begging people all infected with leprosy. The disease still affects close to a quarter of a million people throughout the world, with a majority of these cases in India.

Photo: In Athens, Greece, after one of Master's "talks." He rarely gave a scripted lecture. He spoke in what seemed like a spontaneous way about subjects.

The tour continued to the Ganges River where the group climbed aboard a small boat. Hindus believe that the waters of the Ganges are special, and spiritual in nature. If you go into the river water it will purify your soul.

The river serves as a lifeline for millions of people who live along its course and depend on it for all of their daily needs. John saw many people swimming and bathing in the river, and using it for the tasks of everyday life. He and his companions were quick to determine that they wanted nothing to do with immersing themselves in the polluted waters.

The tour continued on to an ancient building that would serve as an overnight resting spot. In Von Ohlen's words, India was home to the lowest and most tragic and the highest and most opulent. He saw immense poverty, sickness, and people living like animals. But then India is home to the Taj Mahal, spectacular Hindu temples, and spiritual guides such as Maharishi Mahesh Yogi and other great mystics.

The travelers bedded down for the night at a building that resembled a hotel or hostel. The group members enjoyed a welcome shower and good night's rest. The growing interest in India and spiritual "enlightenment" was attracting a diverse collection of travelers, including young people from America. It was the late sixties after all. The ashram was a disgusting mess. John witnessed many of the younger people sleeping and defecating on the surrounding grounds. Master was friendly to these fellow travelers but later that night could be heard cussing a blue streak not at the kids, but the owners. They were supposed to be spiritual leaders and this was an ashram. That they had such little respect was very upsetting.

Later Von Ohlen learned that Master had written a professionally worded letter to the government describing the terrible conditions. Because there was growing interest in cleaning up areas visited by tourists, the site was closed. Sickness and poverty was everywhere in India but there were efforts being made to change that.

The travelers made their way through the squalor of Mumbai and ventured outside the city into an India untouched by modern society. Eventually the group traveled by jeep into the Himalayas. One of the monks, in conversations with a driver, identified a camp area at fourteen thousand feet that would be their destination.

Photo: In Moscow, John is walking front center in with his head looking downward. Master is dressed in white coat and hat as he leads the group. Master was a premier ballet dancer in San Francisco before turning his life over to his calling.

It was as if they were all on an unplanned journey unfolding before their eyes. They drove at night over winding, mountainous roads. John gripped the metal siding as he sat in the back of a jeep, hypnotized by the cliffs plunging thousands of feet straight down just a foot or two from the tires' edges. The drivers continued, completely unnerved by the narrow slice of gravel separating each vehicle from the deathly deep canyons below.

The winding mountainside trail inched upward until it became too narrow for the vehicles to continue. The travelers disembarked from the jeeps and continued by foot, following the guides along a path toward their destination. Monks and Sherpa carried the supplies.

The Sherpa people are elite mountain climbers whose physiology has adapted to the extreme altitudes of the Himalayas. The Himalayas stretch over five countries, but Sherpa live mainly in the Nepal region. They're well known for the important role they play in accompanying expeditions into the Himalayas, especially Mt. Everest.

With every step John felt like he had fifty-pound weights strapped to his boots as he labored up the rocky path. Though exhausted, he was able to complete the last portion with help from a nearby monk.

Travelers in top condition were able to make it on their own, but Von Ohlen wasn't the only one to find the extreme altitudes daunting. When John finally made his way into a cabin he found Master exhausted, already passed out asleep.

At night the temperatures dropped below zero. When dawn arrived, Master told the group he wanted to gather for

meditation. They were at such extreme altitudes that just moving ten steps left John so winded that he needed to sit. But gather they did, and for John the experience was spectacular. Mountain ranges unfolded across the horizon. Mt. Everest appeared like a crown jewel in the distance. The sun rose slowly like a goddess opening her arms with a stunning display of nature. Dark blankets of clouds and developing storms could be seen in one area as clear blue skies embraced the travelers when they gazed elsewhere.

Photo: Moscow: Master front & center with white hat and coat. John is sitting on ground just to his right.

42

For a week members practiced Hatha yoga, meditated, read, talked, and listened to Master. The Sherpa walked about with relative ease, seeing to basic needs like food and keeping fires burning. John had taken another step into an entirely new world. He surrendered, letting go of thoughts about what had been or wondering what might be. Along with this entirely new and evolving spiritual journey, he was left exhausted by the altitude and rugged surroundings.

After the long week and with the help of the Sherpa and monks, the tour slowly began winding along the trail back to the jeeps. Coming from a world of concrete, electricity, and running water, the past seven days were unlike anything John had known.

Photo: Bangalore, India: John looks on as children ride an elephant.

The travelers were all smiles when they arrived back in "civilization" and clamored off the jeeps outside a modern hotel. John felt like he was "waking from the dead." There was laughter and joking all around as tour members walked into rooms that offered showers and beds. Before long Master appeared and verbally exploded. Were the travelers so easily swayed by modern comforts?

Master rarely gave concrete lectures or instructions; the journey was and is a much more subtle experience left for each to draw from. But after the remarkable and simple existence experienced together in the mountains, perhaps Master wanted to remind the travelers they had experienced something so raw, beautiful, and humbling and not to be so easily impressed by having the option of room service or hot running water in their room. Maybe he didn't want them to so quickly forget, and pull from the experience whatever was meant to be.

Photo: Watching the snake charmer. Master explained that when meditating, the meditator gets to this high point like a cobra.

The group traveled on to Bangkok, in central Thailand. Bangkok is home to over forty thousand Buddhist temples. This includes some of the world's most elaborate spectacles visited by thousands of tourists every year, as well as temples hidden away in jungles and rarely seen. The power of what John saw and felt "blew [him] away." The Siamese music and the dancers were another experience like nothing he'd ever known. The dancers surrendered and gave themselves over to unseen magic. They were carried by fluid, unscripted movements and an otherworldly smile on their face and in their eyes. For Von Ohlen, he felt like he was being transported to another reality, away from this planet.

During the tour, Master would sometimes talk about specific topics and religious beliefs. When he spoke there was often no agenda or specific message for John or the others to absorb. Weaved among the discussions was the concept of "self" and "Self" with a capital S, and a chance to reflect about our attachment to our physical bodies.

Master told his followers, "Don't regard me as a person, I am a six-dimensional being in a physical body."

At first John couldn't help but think this pretentious, but over time he realized that Master really was special. Master would talk about being outside his body. He said, "Right now I am doing nothing, nothing—I am just watching."

Today John is selective about who he talks to about this part of his life. Not only is it very personal and difficult to put into words, he's learned that some friends find his description too strange or bizarre. Maybe some of us cling so strongly to a single interpretation of reality that contemplating something radically different is disconcerting. For John, he thrived on the chance to experience the world in very different ways.

Back to That Other World

The drum set had been put away as John devoted himself to time with Master and the world tour. Eventually he set foot back into his world of responsibilities and music, but the spiritual journey never left him. The influence can be heard in his music, both as a player and a teacher. Anyone with a deep sense of the spiritual will carry that essence through whatever they do, certainly in their artwork. A drummer has a style that is natural for him. John believes each of us has our own uniqueness, and if a musician or any individual tries to be something or adopt a style that is not theirs, something special is lost. The journey of discovery is not a finite thing. For John, his philosophy and curiosity for a deeper awareness remain with him still.

After three months of travel with Master, John returned to the United States. He traveled to different cities, picking up gigs and connecting with musicians he'd meet. He was in New York City having a beer and catching up with friend Marvin Stamm, a trumpet player he'd first met in North Texas. Stamm himself has played with a who's who collection of names, including Stan Kenton in the early '60s. Marvin mentioned to John that Urbie Green—the great trombonist—was looking for a drummer. Von Ohlen replied, "Heck, give him a call." Urbie Green is known as the "trombonist's trombonist." He's toured with Woody Herman, Gene Krupa and Frankie Carle. He's played and recorded with Count Basie, Frank Sinatra, Leonard Bernstein, and Louis Armstrong.

After a few minutes on the phone, Stamm returned to the table saying the bandleader wanted to talk to John. A person would be hard pressed to find a more pleasant and laid-back fellow than Urbie. The bandleader asked John about his background and musicians he'd played with. After a few minutes of conversation and with no mention of an audition or trials, Urbie said, "OK, you've got the job." What followed was a six-month tour around the country playing a number of great gigs with Green and his band.

Eventually John gravitated to Las Vegas, where there seemed to be an endless amount of playing opportunities. The hitch was it would take six months to get his union papers. He washed dishes, bused tables, anything that would pay the bills.

It wasn't long before another opportunity knocked: the chance to play with the *Holiday on Ice* traveling big show. Not only was it steady work, there was a strong focus toward a big-band sound and loud, upbeat music. *Holiday on Ice* is not the place to play "sad and subdued." Some of the most talented skaters in the world were part of the troupe. They traveled to cities and filled arenas around the country. The traveling show carried its own rhythm section and always arranged to pull top musicians from every region to complete the orchestra. This usually meant twelve additional horn players and a mallet man for the timpani, xylophone, and bells to join the show in every major city.

The orchestra sounded great. John's drumming was obviously an important part as they played music intended to bring customers to their feet and create a happy, upbeat atmosphere. When not traveling to a new venue they were open for business seven days a week, including two shows on Saturday and three on Sunday. For Von Ohlen, playing with *Holiday on Ice* was loads of fun and a good opportunity. Today, to cut costs, a handful of musicians and recorded music are used to create the same full sound that filled the arenas every day back then.

Growing with Stan

It was now 1970. After traveling and playing with *Holiday on Ice* for a complete season, another opportunity came knocking. Stan Kenton was ready to hit the road and he wanted John on the drums. Over the years he's played with lots of big names and numerous venues, but John would always mark his musical life as before and after Stan. Working with and getting to know Stan Kenton was a life-altering experience.

The band worked just about every night. This meant traveling by bus after a gig and arriving in a new town early the next day. More often than not they'd either be performing at a nightclub or in a university town. The Stan Kenton Orchestra might arrive on campus, set up, and start by playing a thirty-minute set for the student body. Then they'd go into the classrooms and work with members of the school band. After all that, they'd take a break before giving a full concert that same evening. After weeks of this daily grind, John and his bandmates would be running on fumes.

When they were lucky, they'd get a break from highway life and the rigors of endless travel. The orchestra would get off the road and play somewhere like the Tropicana in Las Vegas for thirty days. After a couple of weeks in the same hotel room and eating regular meals, John and his bandmates started to feel human again. The Stan Kenton Orchestra was a hard-living group of guys who enjoyed a special bond courtesy of all that time spent together on the road. They'd drink before and after the show, but it never impacted how they sounded.

The musicians were professionals, and part of their creed was they wouldn't let their extra-curricular behavior interfere with the music. Of course, there are exceptions to most rules. The band bus pulled into in Princeton, New Jersey, for a gig later that day at the esteemed university. By evening the weather had become downright horrendous, with bad storms and trees down. All involved assumed that night's performance had been canceled. Not wanting to see a free bar that had already been set up go to waste, he and his bandmates started drinking—and drinking.

After a couple hours of enjoying the free booze, everyone was sufficiently intoxicated and suddenly surprised to hear the event had not been called off. Of course the show must go on, and man did they stink up the place. John says they sounded awful, and Stan was very angry.

Photo: Rehearsal with the Stan Kenton Orchestra. Stan liked to give his featured players nicknames, thus John became known as "The Baron."

It wasn't long after the Princeton incident that John decided to give up drinking. He'd long recognized a tendency in himself toward excess or extremes, kind of all in or all out.

Living on the road and hanging out with fellow musicians, John was a heavy drinker. After just a few months of traveling with Stan Kenton he decided it was time for drastic measures. When the Stan Kenton Orchestra took a break from the road, John checked into a hotel in Los Angeles and did nothing but lay low in his room and dry out over much of the week. More than ten years would pass before John started to drink again. That would come later, when he started to visit a club called the Blue Wisp Jazz Club.

John consumed a lot of alcohol in those days on the road, but the sober exceptions were his traveling days with Billy Maxted, Woody Herman, and all but three months with Stan Kenton. During all those periods he didn't touch a drop. It's a reflection of his all-or-nothing personality; there doesn't seem to be any middle of the road. He seems to be drawn toward a life of extremes. But he never again would use the harder drugs that were popular with some musicians. Life in music and on the road has claimed countless victims, and John has lost many a friend to such a lifestyle over the years. Just about anything goes or can happen when a group of guys travel the country, drinking, sleeping, and eating on the bus, or with loads of downtime in some roadside motel. No matter what the musicians did to themselves, John always felt the band sounded top-notch. He laughs in describing one of the few unwritten rules they did in fact live by: no women on the bus. The bus was their clubhouse on wheels. One time the trumpet player brought a gal he'd met at a club on board and the usually boisterous group went stone silent. In no time, the poor woman slinked off the bus with the help of the offending bandmate. He was then reminded in no uncertain terms that he had played a bad note.

One of the more memorable experiences with Stan was in Palm Springs, where the Stan Kenton Orchestra had a  series of gigs. Located in the desert of California, Palm Springs was an especially hopping place back then and it was a who's who of big-time names in attendance, including Bob Hope, Bing Crosby, and plenty of other celebrities. The event took place on a golf course with the band positioned on a putting green. Von Ohlen and his drums sat on an elevated platform floating on a small pond behind the green. What made it memorable was no sooner had the music started than the head on his snare broke with no replacement skin anywhere. The comedy of errors continued as John kept the beat on his injured drum set. The pontoon began leaking, with the float dipping to one side and sheets of music sliding into the water. He kept his end of the bargain afloat though, as the band's performance made it across the finish line just in time.

Photo: Playing with Stan Kenton (notice the large cymbals—a requirement in accompanying Kenton's Orchestra).

Life with the Stan Kenton Orchestra continued for almost two years. They traveled throughout the world, including Sweden, England, Germany, and much of Europe. Kenton's Orchestra cut three albums. *Modern Drummer* magazine named John one of the Top-Ten Drummers in the country.

Being a natural showman, Stan often gave his musicians nicknames to make them larger than life. The title "The Baron" originated with Stan Kenton. Older enthusiasts still remember Baron Von Ohlen, or the Baron Von Ohlen Quartet.

When the band did take a break from the road, Stan would return home to Los Angeles. True to his vagabond ways, John would crash in one of the spacious backrooms in Stan's offices. California was home base for the Kenton family. Stan had business ties to Capital Records in addition to recording on the label.

John learned many things watching and listening to his bandleader and friend. This included a greater understanding of the recording and entertainments industries. The music business changed a lot after the '60s, especially with the arrival of the Beatles. In spending time with Stan, John learned that there was a day that record companies—including Capital—devoted resources more equally toward representing different categories of music, including jazz, pop, and classical. EMI, the English division of Capital Records, originally signed the Beatles after Decca turned them down. Decca was so terrified of making such a big mistake again that a year later when they heard a scruffy band named the Rolling Stones, they quickly signed them.

In Stan's words, "the Beatles ruined the business." Nothing against the Fab Four and the entire "British Invasion," but now there was enormous pressure, and focus, to discover the next mega- selling band that appealed to record-buying youngsters. It was the '60s and musical tastes were changing. These trends were affecting what musicians like Von Ohlen had to play to make a living, but more on that later.

In 1972, John was contacted by one of the monks affiliated with Master. Another trip was being organized that would again take the faithful through Europe and the Far East. The monk encouraged John to come along.

Von Ohlen had lived a dream that he'd had since he was fourteen. His whole life changed when he heard the mesmerizing sound of Mel Lewis on drums and those cymbals cutting through the night air as he walked across the parking lot. John kept following that music as he made his way up to that ballroom stage in Indianapolis. It's dramatic but true; he knew that one day he had to play with Stan Kenton's swinging big-band orchestra, and he'd done it. He lived it. Music is such a part of him, and the time with Stan remains one of the highlights of John's life.

When the call came pulling him away from the Big Band, Von Ohlen knew it was time. It's hard to believe it was over forty years ago, but Von Ohlen still remembers it like it was just last week. They were on the road and John approached Stan in the lobby of their hotel. Kenton exploded; he couldn't believe what he was hearing. He was losing his drummer, one of the hottest jazz drummers in the country. As their conversation continued, John stood by his decision to leave. Stan threw up his arms in frustration, turned, and walked away.

John returned to his hotel room, determined to follow through on his plans. He was relieved when a short while later the phone rang. It was Stan. Kenton knew John was a big coffee drinker, and he had a fresh pot in his room. John should come by and they'd talk.

John wanted Stan—who was a mentor and friend—to understand. There was an earlier time that playing with the Stan Kenton Orchestra had been what he wanted more than anything, but John explained that his journey was leading him elsewhere now. They discussed the calling John felt to study other beliefs and religions, and spend more time with Master. Anyone who really gets music understands spiritual journeys. After plenty of coffee and conversation, Stan gave John a pat on the back and his blessings.

They agreed to finish a scheduled tour that lasted another month and would take the Orchestra back to Europe. Check out Kenton's album *Live in London* with John Von Ohlen on drums for further proof of how great the band sounded.

The Journey Continues

John traveled back to Europe and India with Master for three months. As before, there was never any preaching or proselytizing. They practiced Hatha yoga and meditated for hours. The group traveled on while listening, discussing, and exploring assorted beliefs and religions.

John wondered if this second trip would be as powerful for him as the first, and he was not disappointed. Again he immersed himself in the experience. Master expected total devotion from his monks, and while on a tour the same was true of his followers.

To this day, John vividly remembers one collection of events. Earlier they had attended a Ganesha festival. Lord Ganesha is one of the best-known and loved deities in the Hindu pantheon of Gods. Ganesha is represented in slightly different forms but always has the head of an elephant, usually a big belly, and four arms. He is the Lord of Good Fortune who provides prosperity, fortune, and success. He is the Lord of Beginnings and the Remover of Obstacles—both material and spiritual. Interestingly, he also places obstacles in the path of those who need to be checked. Devotees believe that if Ganesha is worshiped, he grants success, prosperity, and protection against adversity. When Hindus build a bridge or take on any endeavor, they pray to Ganesha for success.

Master and his followers were at an ancient Indian temple relaxing, meditating, and practicing yoga. Yoga did not come easily to John physically, but it was an important part of the practice. As he sat in silence, the vibes John felt were subtle but overwhelming. He began to leave his physical body. He surrendered to a wave of gentle submissiveness. Not as in weakness, but simply that he had no will of his own. It is and is not a deeper awareness, because being aware implies thinking and the experience is actually one of no thought, no self-narration or judgment. In his own words, "Ganesha got [me] and that is still with [me]." This experience with Ganesha is one of the most profound experiences he's ever felt. He was taken over and felt surrounded by the presence of Ganesha and of love. It was an experience that was "religious in nature," and he prays to Ganesha every day.

This second tour would be the last time he would visit with Master in person, but they kept in contact by phone and talked every week for over twenty years. Master possessed "darshan," a holy charisma or aura. The darshan John experienced that day was like a vibration that moved John closer to discovering the singularity of God and Self.

Not long after returning to Indianapolis, John would have another intense and incredibly profound experience. He'd been driving his car fast when he pulled to a stop at a red light. Since returning, John had been devoted to concentrating on his practice and what Master's teachings said. As he sat at the intersection the sensation flooded over him: *he was watching himself watch himself.* He knew he had always been and always would be. This was not an intellectual thought—it just took him. John's earlier experience with Ganesha had been *religious*. What he felt this day he calls "yogic in nature." Call it a sensation, experience, transformative, whatever— he carries with him the religious and the yogic every day.

Even now, every part of his life is affected as he tries to open himself to experiencing the universe, and what spiritual means to him. John's beliefs manifest in his playing and in teaching other musicians. Anyone who has seen him play can't help but be struck by the way he follows his own instincts, his own inner drummer. At his best he is totally present each time he hits a drum or creates a sound; it is a unique sound unlike any other in the universe. He coaches others to do the same, to respect and listen to their own unique instincts and create the beat that is unique to them. To be in the moment and not try to be something they are not.

Master said do what you do naturally, it will open and unfold, and you will shape your life direction and work out of it then. You will move in a direction toward being completed and fulfilled. By following and listening to your inner instincts, the path will become clear. There are so many noises, distractions, and ways to go numb that silence what the universe is shaping us to be. We drown out our specialness. Master believes all this was finished—completed long, long ago. The natural "you" happens, and we must do our best to pay attention to that natural message as part of our journey.

Following this second experience traveling with Master in 1972, John moved back to Indianapolis. A steady diet of life on the road had become tiresome and although still drawn to growing and exploring music, success at any price had lost its luster. "Name and fame" did not hold the same power over his life that it once had. John had lost interest in touring and extensive studio work. He wanted to play his music for the people who enjoyed hearing it.

John started to plant the seeds to grow more permanent roots around Indianapolis. To satisfy his desire for a simpler life, he found a place in the country. Bobby Milligan, a trumpet player and friend in New York City, told John he should contact Bobby's father about a place to live. Mr. Milligan was a farmer who owned some apartments next to an old bait shop outside Indianapolis. The building was located close to an area that would be called a nature preserve today. Most of John's life had been spent in cities surrounded by concrete, noise, and the faster pace found in urban areas. It was living above the old bait shop that would help him find the solitude and quiet that he craved.

Over time, John slowly started to reacquaint himself with the local music scene, but he also spent full days on his own, rediscovering the drums. He would spend an entire day focusing on sound; exploring the vibrations he could pull from different areas of a cymbal or drumhead. Percussion is a mysterious journey of sound. His focus was not so much on drum riffs; rather, John wanted to toy with what portion of a cymbal generates a desired sound or the impact of drumhead tension. He was fascinated by the nuances, and to this day he works with different touches and techniques to create unique or desired sounds.

One way John paid the bills during this time was teaching. He discovered enjoyment and fulfillment in a way he hadn't previously considered. After playing with musicians who'd spent years perfecting their art, John started instructing young children on the very basics of percussion. Working with youngsters who were sometimes no older than seven or eight meant focusing on things such as how to hold a drumstick and striking a snare drum in different places on the skin head. Both teacher and student enjoyed the experience, and John got to revisit the most fundamental aspects of drumming. There was no focus on complicated sticking patterns or other advanced techniques. As a professional, John has traveled the country, given clinics, and mentored older and advanced musicians who already have their own styles and expectations. Some of his fondest teaching memories are working with these curious youngsters years ago.

After a few months, John began to explore the music scene in Indianapolis. He went to hear pianist Claude Sifferlen. Claude and John were friends from high school and were also bandmates in the Woody Herman Orchestra. Sifferlen was developing his own impressive resume of musical experiences, including later sitting in for Stan Kenton.

Claude was playing with a young musician named Steve Allee. Allee would go on to play piano with a who's who of talent including the Buddy Rich Orchestra, Jeff Hamilton, and Ed Thigpen. Another talent of Steve's would prove to be as an arranger, composing for orchestras like the Stan Kenton Orchestra as well as creating soundtracks for television and film. Kenton called Allee one of the best young talents in the country. John was amazed later when he would tell Steve about a musical idea and Steve would return in a few days with the charts. In 2001, John would rejoin Allee as part of the Steve Allee Orchestra on the Grammy-nominated big-band record, *Downtown Blues*.

The two musicians were creating their own unique sound. Claude played acoustic and electric piano with Steve on organ, and some electric piano while laying down a strong bass sound. In no time, John knew he wanted to work with the two and be a part of the music. The three played together a few times and decided a vocalist would be the perfect complement for their sound.

John had just the right person in mind. Mary Ann Moss was singing and living in St. Louis. What he wanted was not simply someone to sing straight lyrics; he also wanted someone to add inflections and play with vocals to create sounds. He contacted Mary Ann and agreed to drive to Missouri and move her and her assorted belongings to Indianapolis. As a result, we have the Baron Von Ohlen Quartet and one of the more satisfying periods in John's musical life.

The group—the Baron Von Ohlen Quartet Featuring Mary Ann Moss—produced one album, *The Baron*. When the quartet cut the album, they figured its appeal would be limited to the local market courtesy of the gigs they were playing around Indianapolis. When Stan Kenton was in town and got a listen, he had other ideas. Ever the marketer with an ear for talent, Stan convinced the quartet to let him promote the album throughout the United States and parts of Europe, where it sold well. Stan also asked John if he was interested in returning to Stan's band, but Von Ohlen said he was enjoying himself too much and felt committed to this new endeavor.

Mary Ann gave their music a pop flavor when necessary, which was an added bonus—especially for live performances. The music world was changing, and her vocals gave the quartet added versatility. Mary Ann would keep the radio on throughout the day, listening for popular songs she thought the other three wouldn't find too distasteful. When she came across a tune, she'd bring it to the guys and they'd play around with various interpretations and see what they could come up with. This way, they'd satisfy customers looking for what was popular on the radio while still mixing in the music that fed their musical souls.

The music was good and the band was hot. They kept busy playing local gigs six nights a week. John likened the sound to the old George Shearing Quintet, only with electronic keyboards. The musicians called the band "George Shearing on Acid." The Baron Von Ohlen Quartet created a unique kind of harmony, and Mary Ann would add just the right touch of vocals. The quartet played locally with limited travel for almost two years. It was the '70s and there was a shift taking place with what the public was looking for, but it was a health issue John had been battling that sadly put an end to the quartet.

The problem had nothing to do with bad habits. John hadn't been a drinker since those early months with Stan Kenton. The health problem that sidelined John was one that is common with the jazz and big-band guys. Many musicians suffer from damage to their hearing, often including a condition known as tinnitus, a persistent ringing in the ears. Thanks to the popularity of the quartet, they'd been playing six days a week and close to five hours a night. They played at full volume and he was subjected to loud, heavy-duty electronic music almost daily. Looking back, he says they probably went overboard playing so often, but he was having too much fun.

The tinnitus became so loud and distracting that John had to do something. It seemed especially bad because of all the buzzing and white noise created by the intense electronics of the music. It broke his heart, but this was the end of the Baron Von Ohlen Quartet. Maybe the reason John was so bothered by the never-ending sounds in his ears was because he had become much more attuned to his body. He'd been meditating and sitting in silence for years.

John kept playing his music, without such a heavy emphasis on amplifiers and electronics. Like many musicians, John was still surrounded by the obnoxious buzzing sound in his ears, but a professional just learns to block it out. After a life filled with high-volume, big-band music, it's a wonder John can still hear, but escaping that constant electric buzzing of the quartet might have lowered the distracting noise in his ears just a notch.

Before long, John went back to something he loved and put together a big-band orchestra. He enjoyed the two-keyboard sound so much that he made sure to include Steve and Claude. The Big Band played together one night a week for almost eight years. With changing tastes, the venues also would change. For a time, the Big Band even played in rock 'n' roll clubs. As long as they played loud, the crowd liked it.

Playing with the Big Band stood out as the weekly gig that he looked forward to. The challenge was what to do for work the rest of the week. As the '70s rolled on, the music the public wanted continued to change, and that was certainly the case in Indianapolis. There were only so many gigs for the orchestra. To pay the bills, John and the other musicians were forced to play anything from bar mitzvahs to car shows. Rock 'n' roll had swept the land, and that's what audiences wanted, so John adapted.

Time for Another Change

John grew more and more tired of the heavy diet of pop music he was playing. His heart was still in big band and jazz, playing with musicians who spoke his language. He eventually said, "No, can't do it," when the phone rang with another offer to play music that wasn't his thing. Nothing against those who play acid rock, Top 40, or primarily at bar mitzvahs and birthdays—John's musical interests were too strong for him to ignore. Following inner truths had become a very loud voice in his life.

While the scene in Indianapolis seemed to be fading, a few hours away Cincinnati was vibrating with his kind of music. A friend and bass player by the name of Bud Hunt contacted John about a gig at the old Buccaneer Lounge on Reading Road. The place was a smoke-filled cave, and John felt right at home. The gig was with Bud and one of the best guitarists around, a fellow by the name of Cal Collins. The trio sounded great. There was even an old hotel behind the lounge and John could crash there at no charge rather make the long drive home at some ungodly late hour. The Buccaneer Lounge is long gone now, but if those walls could still carry a tune they'd be singing about the great music and good times that took place inside. Old timers tell stories of when the doors would lock at closing and entertainers such as Mel Tormé and Mark Murphy—who arrived following a paying gig elsewhere—would take the stage at the Buccaneer Lounge for a late-night jam.

Collins and John became fast friends, and man could Cal *play*. The guitarist was another free-spirited character who was persistent in telling John he should move closer to Cincinnati, saying there were plenty of gigs around the area. It was 1978 when John gave in and rented an old farmhouse in Sunman, Indiana, midway between the two cities. True to form for Von Ohlen, it was a simple place that he got dirt-cheap, but it was enough for his few possessions. It brought the drummer closer to Cincinnati and Northern Kentucky. When he told Collins, the guitarist responded in his enthusiastic style, "Yeah darling, come on."

One day Bud called John to tell him about a change. Cal had taken a gig with Benny Goodman and they'd have a temporary sub on guitar. As far as Von Ohlen was concerned, there was only one Cal Collins and he told Bud to "forget it." He wasn't interested in loading his drums into the car and making the trip. "Wait man," said Hunt, "he's a great guitarist. You're gonna like this guy." John made the drive, and the young guitarist was fantastic. When John heard his distinctive style, he immediately thought of friend and legendary session player George Van Eps (John used to listen to Van Eps play the guitar for hours). The guitarist sitting in for Cal that night was Kenny Poole.

Now that John had moved closer to the Queen City, he figured the next step was to start hitting a few area clubs. He needed more work than one night a week at the Buccaneer Lounge. He had few contacts and wasn't familiar with the music scene around the city. With Cal doing his own thing and touring with Benny Goodman, Von Ohlen was starting from scratch. There was an old tavern called the Blue Wisp Jazz Club he'd heard about. The Blue Wisp had developed a reputation as a home for good jazz. A number of future Cincinnati legends performed there and knocked back many a drink or three at the bar.

The Blue Wisp was located in an older neighborhood called O'Bryonville, just a couple miles from downtown Cincinnati. Built in the early 1900s, the Blue Wisp was nothing fancy, but the wooden interior was a good place for music. When John first visited and got a listen to Jimmy McGary and Pat Kelly jamming, he knew it was his kind of place.

There are different opinions about when Paul and Marjean Wisby bought the Blue Wisp, but it's safe to say it was sometime in the mid-to-late 1970s. A fellow named Harry Garrison had a well-known piano store next door. Paul Wisby was a country boy and he planned to offer country music, true to his roots. Fortunately, Harry convinced Paul that what would make a name for the Blue Wisp was becoming a home for jazz. Harry even donated a nine-foot Steinway.

Meltdown of Another Sort

After visiting places like the Blue Wisp, John was meeting people and spreading the word that he was looking for work. It was early 1979. Before anything had come together locally, John got a call about a regular out-of-town job with Steve Rudolph, the composer and jazz pianist. Steve had created a hopping jazz scene with top New York talent in Harrisburg, Pennsylvania. It was good money and steady work six nights a week, so Von Ohlen packed his gear and headed east. He called Harrisburg his second home for three months until an accident at a nuclear power plant. For folks old enough to remember, the entire country stood at a standstill, transfixed to see what might happen at Three Mile Island during what newscasters and experts alike called a nuclear meltdown. Smoke poured from Reactor #2 as the world watched and wondered if we were witnessing one of the worst nuclear accidents in history. Reporters, government officials, and military personnel poured into town as John watched the events unfolding not far from the window of his tenth-floor hotel room.

The town was on the verge of chaos while the National Guard kept order and the locals looked on, terrified and wondering what was next. Worried about getting caught up in some mass evacuation. John told Rudolph, "I'm outta here," and bought a ticket on the first train headed toward Cincinnati. He didn't learn until seated on board that the railroad cars he was traveling on went right past the nuclear plant.

When John got home to his small hideaway on the farmland of Indiana, one of the first things he did was make the short walk to the lake out back. It was early springtime and nature was working its magic. Gusts of wind danced across the water kicking up white caps, surrounded by open fields and a large expanse of trees in the distance. John sat down in the wild grass and filled his lungs with the clean country air, more convinced than ever that he'd had enough of hotel rooms and traveling from one gig to another. True to his word, he's had to have a good reason to hit the road ever since.

Putting Down Roots—Assorted People and Stories

Cal Collins

Once back in Sunman, it wasn't long before Cal Collins contacted John about work at Gilly's in Dayton. It was spring 1979 and Cal had a standing gig, so Von Ohlen would make the drive of close to two hours north just about every night from his farmhouse to the club. Collins was one of the best, and John played numerous gigs with him over the years. He reminisces that playing with Cal was like witnessing a sunrise. His guitar playing could take your breath away.

Along with the long drive to Dayton, the evening sometimes proved to be an adventure in other ways. Like many artist and musicians, Cal was a free spirit. But he was special in that at times he'd take it to a whole new level. There were occasions that John didn't know what Cal would play as John sat back on the drums trying to figure out what was next. Often this involved Cal's imbibing in numerous alcoholic beverages. Cal just loved to play guitar, so he'd "go [off] the deep end" with the other musicians while trying to figure out where he was headed on his guitar.

Dee Felice

In recent years, John and the Von Ohlen Trio have enjoyed a standing gig just blocks from his home at the Dee Felice Café in Covington, Kentucky. Practically an institution, the restaurant was opened by Dee in the '80s. Another good friend of John's, Dee Felice, was a talented and well-known drummer in his own right. Sadly, he passed away not long after the Cajun-themed club opened. Dee's wife Shirley and daughter Shelly took over and have managed it successfully for years. They've provided a musical home for John and offered the public a steady diet of quality live jazz. Dee's café has also been a welcoming venue for young jazz artists. John smiles when remembering that Dee would give his musician friends free booze. Once the ladies stepped in they ran a tight ship, including no open bar for musicians. John says the café would never have lasted all these years with Dee's generosity.

Kenny Poole

Kenny Poole was a "guitarist's guitarist." Similar to George Van Eps, Kenny tuned his guitar low and had a unique picking style while weaving together the chords into a distinct sound. The man was a genius and could play literally any tune requested. Cal and Kenny had completely different styles, but they would perform together often over the years as a guitar duo. To this day, John can't believe that two of the best guitarists in the country lived here in Cincinnati.

In the 1980s, Kenny had a regular gig at the Celestial up on the hill in Cincinnati. He asked John to back him. Kenny's unique style was magical and he was especially good at bossa nova. Poole was a quiet man who did his talking through his music, and he was the first to tell friends he could be quite moody. Kenny warned John early on that sometimes he would fall into a dark and sullen place.

The gig was steady work four or five nights a week in the upstairs lounge. John would accompany the guitarist with a stripped-down set of snare, bass drum, hi-hat, and cymbal. Drummers sometimes place a napkin, towel, or other object on a drumhead to muffle the sound. When he played this gig with Kenny in the Celestial's upstairs lounge, Von Ohlen would put a phonebook on the snare. Looking back, the story takes on special meaning because it was the only time John was fired from a gig. Kenny was having a bad night, in a sullen and dark mood. He started in on John, giving him all sorts of grief about his playing. He just kept barking at him about doing this or that wrong. Von Ohlen finally decided he'd had enough. John broke down his set, slammed the heavy phonebook on the floor in disgust, and walked out. John was out of a job, replaced by the talented Terry Moore.

The Cymbal

When John made the move to Sunman in the fall of 1978, it only took one trip. A few pots and plates, his clothes, books, and phonograph records were wedged around his drum set in the car. Breaking down and lugging a drum set from place to place gets tiresome. The basics include hi-hat stand, bass pedal, stool, snare stand and snare, ride cymbals, crash, splash, hi-hat cymbals, hanging toms, floor tom, bass, and various sticks and brushes. Talented drummers like Von Ohlen don't need a multitude of percussion toys to get the sounds they want. A good drummer can do fine with a simple set as long as it is tuned to his liking. The cymbal is another thing. The audience or uninitiated may assume all cymbals sound alike. Nothing could be further from the truth, and a drummer, especially a jazz guy, could spend a lifetime looking for a cymbal with just the sound he wants.

Proof of the high priority John placed on getting the perfect sound he wanted from his drumming is evident in a discovery he made when traveling with Woody Herman. In 1967, Herman's band stopped in Cincinnati for a show at a club called the Living Room. Von Ohlen knew next to nothing about the city back then. Across the street from the club was a music store owned by Ray Lammers. The store was stocked with every kind of musical instrument, from saxophones to piccolos to violin bows. Tacked to the wall were row upon row of cymbals, from mini splash to enormous rides, from bright shining silver to dark-grained and copper-colored. More than one hundred cymbals of every size and shape wallpapered the walls of the store. John was in cymbal heaven.

Like most jazz drummers, he was a cymbal fanatic. Jazz is about bebop, swinging, and riding on the cymbals. Rock 'n' roll has much more emphasis on drums, keeping time on a cymbal, and crashes for punctuation. A drummer playing what is broadly referred to as "jazz" could have a certain sound in mind for years before he finds just the right cymbal. John certainly did.

Photo: Playing with the Blue Wisp Big Band (notice the "bites" cut out of the large cymbal).

The first Zildjian cymbals were made in 1618. One of the oldest companies in the world, Zildjian was the first to develop drum-set cymbals with names such as ride, crash, and hi-hat. For decades, he company has supplied the top drummers in the world. Lammers was friends with Avedis Zildjian of the Zildjian cymbal company out of Boston. Avedis would send Ray cymbals at no charge every couple of weeks.

Von Ohlen couldn't believe what he'd walked into, but he told Ray that he couldn't use them. The plates had been tacked or nailed to a wall. No sooner had John spoken these words of disappointment about the damaged cymbals than the store owner gestured toward a staircase. Following the long column of steps upward, John walked into a large attic room and was in for another big surprise.

What he saw were racks and more racks of cymbals. Many wore a heavy coat of dust, but were in great condition. John has always believed that Zildjians from the '40s and '50s are some of the best jazz cymbals made. Like Indiana Jones discovering the Holy Grail, John eyed a twenty-six-inch cymbal and gingerly slid it out from the heavy stack. Most cymbals are no more than twenty-two inches in diameter, so this one was enormous. He placed the cymbal on a stand and hit it just once with a drumstick. "Yeah, I can play this," he thought.

Von Ohlen paid one hundred dollars for the cymbal. Expensive in those days, but nothing compared to what a similar cymbal would cost today. The cymbal had a "heavy ping sound" that he didn't think would fit with Woody's band, so John dropped it off for safekeeping at his father's house. He had become ever more focused on sounds. He knew what he wanted when driving or accompanying different music. He knew where the sound from that twenty-six-inch ride cymbal would fit, and he was right.

It wouldn't fit with Woody's band, the Young Thundering Herd, but it would work for the power of the Stan Kenton Orchestra. Years later with Stan Kenton he played that cymbal night after night.

When he hit the road with Stan in 1970, the cymbal went with him and he "beat the heck out of it" from jazz joints to college campuses. Later in his life, after traveling and studying with Master, he became even more conscious of different sounds he could pull from his drum set. Playing with different tensions on a drumhead, cross sticking, accents, sticks, brushes, and more. And to Von Ohlen's well-trained ear, every cymbal has a distinct set of sounds, not much different from the uniqueness of a fingerprint.

Over the years it wasn't unusual for the mammoth cymbal to develop a crack, something that can spell disaster. John found a guy in Denver who could repair the cymbal and preserve the sound. The craftsman knew just where and how to cut a small piece out of the cymbal and thus remove the crack. Over time the cymbal had chunks or what looked like a number of bites taken out of it, but it still sounded sweet.

Remember how the cymbal had stories to tell? Fast forward to when John was still thinking about moving closer to Cincinnati in late 1978. He received a call to do the Sandler & Young show in the Queen City. The orchestra was top-notch, with some of the best musicians in the area such as Don Johnson, Al Nori, and Rudy Minnetti.

Once they started to rehearse, Von Ohlen just knew he belonged; it felt "so right." These guys were so good; it was jazz the way he wanted to play it. During a break from playing, Al Nori walked by the still-new-to-the-scene drummer and without even blinking an eye the trumpet player said, "What, a dinosaur been scarfing on your cymbal, man?" In the world of hungry musicians, "scarf" means foods on the table. For Von Ohlen it was more confirmation that he was with his kind. He thought to himself, "Man, I gotta move down here cause these are my people."

The Blue Wisp House Band

Not long after the Three Mile Island adventure in the summer of 1979, John got a call from a bass player named Alex Cirin. They had both played with Woody Herman in earlier days, but had never met. Alex introduced himself and explained he was part of the new house band at the Blue Wisp Jazz Club. The current drummer wasn't working out, and Alex asked if Von Ohlen was interested. It was steady work five nights a week with Cirin on bass and a young pianist named Steve Schmidt. They were called the Steve Schmidt Trio. The other two wanted to change the name to Baron Von Ohlen's Trio, but John said a name focusing on the pianist was the way to go.

Photo: The original three (left to right): Michael Sharfe, Steve Schmidt, and John, standing in front of the original Blue Wisp Jazz Club in O'Bryonville. The Steve Schmidt Trio is still together more than thirty-five years later.

Within a couple of months, Alex got into an argument with owner Paul Wisby and walked out. Michael Sharfe, another young and talented musician, joined the trio on bass. It worked, and the Steve Schmidt Trio with Michael, John, and Steve can still be heard making great music today. Sharfe, another staple in the Cincinnati jazz scene, has since played with Michael Feinstein, Manhattan Transfer, the Pops, and often played bass for Rosemary Clooney.

Paul and Marjean Wisby knew next to nothing about jazz, but before long they realized this club was reaching a clientele that went beyond the neighborhood barflies who had called the tavern home. The Blue Wisp would go on to develop an international reputation for quality jazz. And yes, if those old wooden walls could talk, the stories told in addition to the music played would fill volumes. It wasn't unusual for the doors to lock up at closing time but the good times to swing and stagger on 'til sunup. The musicians were in charge of the music, but Marjean held court behind the bar in her own unique and spirited fashion. John chuckles and shakes his head when thinking back to the good times and great music that went on there.

Von Ohlen credits pianist Steve Schmidt for helping the Blue Wisp develop into an internationally known spot for jazz. The owners had limited funds, and Steve worked overtime to bring in musicians while keeping expenses down. Those were in the days when People Express Airlines offered tickets for less than one hundred dollars. Schmidt would offer up his home for out-of-town performers while he stayed at his girlfriend's place. Whatever it took to get big-name talent into town, Steve would work all the angles in finding ways to make it happen.

His goal was half local talent and half out-of-town. For fourteen years, from 1979 until 1993, he devoted himself to getting headliners to visit the club. Paul Wisby passed away in 1984, but Marjean had been in charge of many details and she and Steve continued to work to bring talent into town. Steve's efforts were a big reason why jazz fans from around the country had the Blue Wisp on their short list of places to go when visiting Cincinnati.

The Wisp became known as a home for top-notch jazz players, and the collection of artists that came to town and played the there is a testimony to this reputation. Steve arranged to have trumpeter Johnny Coles, known as "Little Johnny C," visit Cincinnati and the Wisp on more than one occasion. In his career, Coles played with a remarkable list of performers including Gil Evans, Miles Davis, Charles Mingus, Duke Ellington, and Ray Charles.

The house band was usually Schmidt on piano, Michael Sharfe or Lynn Seaton on bass, and John on drums. Because of the wide variety of visiting musicians, the house trio always had to be ready with their best musical chops. The trio was not backing up an entertainer but playing right along with the out-of-town talent. The three musicians entered the creative and musical universe of the featured artist that given night. In addition to Coles, the trio played with saxophonist Scott Hamilton, Mark Murphy, Bud Shank, Joe Lovano, Charlie Rouse, and Clifford Jordan. After years with Oscar Peterson, guitarist Herb Ellis played the Blue Wisp more than once.

Trumpeter Art Farmer traveled in from New York City to play the Wisp, as did a young Fred Hersch. A visitor not easily forgotten was Sun Ra and his band. Sun Ra believed he grew up on another planet, but all records indicate he was from Chicago and part of the jazz scene there as a young musician. He was a composer, and played the piano and synthesizer. He was also a poet and philosopher, and his music could be an adventure. Sun Ra would bring his own band and when the groove was just right, a dancer moved about with lit torch in hand. When the night was at an end the band would wave goodbye playing "Zip-a-Dee-Doo-Dah."

When the rent got too steep in 1989, the Wisp moved from their original location on Madison Road. The new home was downtown Cincinnati and a place that still resembled what a respectable jazz club should be. Located below street level, the clouds of smoke could bring tears to your eyes if the music didn't. There were regulars drinking at the bar who looked like they hadn't seen the sun in days. Marjean did her best to keep the tradition going until her death in 2006. Under new ownership, the club's doors managed to remain open for nearly ten more years. After relocating a couple more times, the Blue Wisp Jazz Club officially bolted their doors for what appears to be the last time in 2014.

Over the years the club was a who's who of people enjoying the good times and good jazz. Members of the Clooney family, including Rosemary, Nick and Nina, or George might be seen tableside, along with Tony Bennett, Mel Tormé, Mark Murphy, Leo Underhill, and various musicians from the Cincinnati Symphony Orchestra. It was a popular place for music and fun after a paid gig with the Cincinnati Pops, Beverly Hills Supper Club, or elsewhere.

It's no surprise that the owner of a jazz club in Cincinnati worried about generating enough cash to pay the bills. Sadly it is the nature of the business, and Paul and Marjean Wisby were no exception. The owners were always on the lookout for a way to save a buck. One day, John told Marjean that there was plenty of exceptional talent living in the city and the club didn't need to keep paying to bring in musicians from around the country. As a result, the club began taking advantage of the local talent more. As he looks back, John can't help but wonder if the downside of his suggestion was the pay scale was tightened for what he and the veterans were making too.

The Big Band Gets Its Start

In the 1970s, a person couldn't live in Cincinnati without knowing the name Bob Braun. Bob took over the *50-50 Club* when Ruth Lyons retired in 1967. The *50-50 Club*, with Ms. Lyons as the host, was originally broadcast on radio as the *50 Club* because she would have fifty women in attendance. When it expanded to one hundred, the name changed to the *50-50 Club*. Her program made the switch to television in 1949. As anyone familiar with those times knows, Ruth was extremely popular with advertisers and

fans in the region. She retired in 1967 and her sidekick Bob Braun assumed the on-air reins of the *50-50 Club*. Bob was one of Cincinnati's biggest television stars until he retired in 1984. The program featured singers and a live band. In 1980, John was sitting in for the regular guy on drums. After the show that day, Von Ohlen went out for beers with Don Johnson, a top-notch trumpet player in Braun's band.

Photo: Front row, left to right: Herb Aronoff (founding member), Steve Hoskins, Brent Gallaher, and Joe Gaudio (founding member).

He and Don agreed they wanted to pull together a Big Band. Johnson would be responsible for the horn section because he knew the top players in town.

Von Ohlen approached Paul and Marjean at the Blue Wisp Jazz Club. Wednesdays were slow, so he suggested to Paul that they play that night. A bigger challenge was Don explaining to the union that the band would not be getting paid scale. He petitioned the union to allow the band to play cheap, receiving only what they made for cover charge at the door. At first the union was adamant in responding, "permission not granted—no go." These were some top-notch musicians. Johnson convinced the rep by explaining they didn't figure the gig would last any longer than a month.

The band rehearsed in the back of a music store a few times and it felt good. In John's words, a "Big Band can be an animal that's hard to control," but this band swung by

itself. Members of the Big Band agreed that not holding more than a few rehearsals was smart. They didn't argue, things, or otherwise mess it up.

Photo: John at a recording session in Cincinnati.

In no time, Wednesdays at the Wisp were hopping. The place was filled as area jazz fans discovered what was happening at the club in O'Bryonville. John wanted to give the band a name that associated it with Cincinnati, but Paul Wisby had a different plan. When introducing the musicians, the owner told the crowd it was the club's band, and so began the Blue Wisp Big Band. As noted, the Blue Wisp locked the doors for what appears to be the last time some thirty-five years later, but the Big Band always seems to find another home. New converts keep discovering their music, while older fans follow the band to their latest

Blue Wisp Big Band

venue. The Blue Wisp Big Band always lands somewhere and keeps swinging. By now, playing together is a part of the contributing musicians' DNA. There has been some turnover, but the majority of players have been with the Blue Wisp Big Band for decades. The guys have provided a welcoming opportunity for talented young players to sit in and play with the best.

Photo: The Blue Wisp Big Band.

None of the original musicians would be offended to acknowledge that, like all people, Father Time has had his way with them. The guys are thankful to still get together one night a week for a few laughs and great music. Over the years, the Big Band has collected a wealth of memories.

In the early 1980s, a man and woman began to appear with regularity at the Wisp. At first they seemed to be just another couple hooked on the swinging sounds of the Blue Wisp Big Band. Like clockwork, the couple would grab a table in the back of the club every week and settle in for an evening's worth of musical entertainment.

Then one night, a surprising thing happened. After the last note had been played and Von Ohlen thanked the crowd, Fred and Helen Morr approached the small stage and introduced themselves. In no time the couple was explaining how they thought the whole show could be improved.

Photo: Jim Sherrick, one of the founding members, takes a solo on the saxophone.

Needless to say, John, Schmidt, and others were caught a bit off-guard by the couple, but their enthusiasm, including suggestions about financial support, was a bit infectious. Fred was a wealthy man and Helen was a charming and attractive woman.

John reminisces that back in the early days it was challenging to get some of his fellow musicians to show up on a regular and predictable basis. Most had other commitments and the Wednesday night gathering was purely for enjoyment; it certainly wasn't for the money.

Having an enthusiastic benefactor in the Morrs was a change, especially when one was the good-looking, leggy, and charming Helen who could now be found sitting front-row center. The band members started showing up with greater regularity.

Photo: John and bassist Michael Sharfe in the groove.

Fred and Helen were supportive and passionate about the music. There was a new buzz around the band, to the point that some members—including John—even felt a bit of concern as to who was in charge. The Morrs were free spirits. They were not married and were very open-minded when it came to their relationship. Eventually Helen and Fred were legally married, with a celebration at the Wisp and entertainment provided by the Blue Wisp Big Band. It was a cheerful event with a smiling and supportive cast.

The Morrs were dedicated to the Big Band, and over time Fred, and especially Helen, had greater influence over the group.
Helen would put together packets for each musician filled with assorted clippings and reviews pulled  from newspapers and trade magazines. The Morrs financed the cost of producing four records by the Big Band. Helen worked hard to see that the albums were marketed around the country and even in Europe. Thanks to her efforts—and the talents of the Blue Wisp Big Band—they garnered some stellar reviews.

Photo: Break time for a young John Von Ohlen.

In 1984, the Morrs paid to fly the entire Blue Wisp Big Band to Los Angeles for a weeklong gig at Carmelo's Jazz Club in Sherman Oaks. The gigs were professionally recorded and eventually marketed as the Blue Wisp Big Band: *Rollin' with Von Ohlen and Live at Carmelo's*. Fred and Helen made sure the entire experience, including lodging and travel, was first class. They invested well over thirty thousand dollars in the trip and recording.

This went on for a few years, but by the mid-'80s the Morrs moved on to other things in their lives and another chapter in the history of the Blue Wisp Big Band came to a close. Since the days of Helen and Fred, the Big Band has cut a couple more records when some of the musicians have pulled together enough cash to cover the costs.

Anyone who's heard these recordings knows they're live, and usually take place at the Blue Wisp Jazz Club. Years of experience in the business have led John to have strong opinions about how to reproduce the best sound. He's adamant that technology, with too many bells and whistles, can ruin what ends up on the record. He says, "Place a couple of microphones in front of the band and record." Too often, engineers want to place a microphone next to every drum, directly in front of each musician. This distorts the sound and produces nothing that resembles the full sound of the music being played. Acoustic sound needs airspace to develop. Music is a merging and collecting of sound. A listener doesn't put their ear up against a piano or a drum, and a recording shouldn't sound that way either.

Von Ohlen grew up in the music business when tubes and the importance of airspace for a fuller sound were standard. In his opinion, some of the most memorable acoustic jazz recordings were made in the 1950s. The listener heard the natural sound of brushes whispering across a snare, coming together with bass, piano, and horns. He thinks that one of the best recordings he ever played on was in 1960 with the College All-Stars, recorded in Chicago at Universal Studios using simple microphone techniques.

The change from tubes to transistors may have had a big and negative impact on recording. Another major factor was the explosion of rock 'n' roll. Because the instruments are generally electric, each one goes through an amplifier. The engineer controls and emphasizes the marriage of individual sounds merging together to create the music the fans want.

Photo: Break time, a few years later.

Rosemary Clooney

John checked his answering machine and the recorded voice asked if he was interested in playing Beef & Boards Dinner Theatre in his hometown of Indianapolis. He didn't get many of other details, but sure, he phoned back to say his schedule was open. John didn't know the singer was Rosemary Clooney.

"Best" in music, just like fine wines or forms of creative expression, is in part a subjective discussion influenced by personal tastes. Then there is the role that Lady Luck and timing play in who is selected as the best, whose name ends up on the marquee labeled as "Star." For example, there is the role both talent and good fortune played with Betty and Rosemary Clooney. It's a good bet that with her talent, Rosemary was destined for the big time no matter what. But when it came to luck, what would have happened if the sisters didn't get on that bus to visit WLW? The story goes that the girls had to decide whether they'd spend the only money they had on an ice cream or bus fare. Fortunately, the teens decided to use their last bit of pocket change to travel to an audition at the Cincinnati radio station in 1945. From there it was talent and hard work. The rest is history when it comes to the life and stardom of Rosemary Clooney.

For John, it was a pure delight playing behind Rosemary that summer night in 1983. *Man*, could she swing, and the supporting cast of musicians was top-notch, some of the best in Indianapolis. He had a great time playing and sharing the stage with such a talent. But he figured the gig was one and done.

Only John and Rosie weren't done. In a few weeks he was contacted to do another show. Next thing he knew, he was in the band room with the other musicians getting ready for show time when the door opened and in walked Rosemary Clooney. With no words spoken, she approached the drummer and gave him a big hug, and then with a simple wave to the other musicians, she left. As the silence became louder, John looked around at his bandmates, and they were all a bit bug-eyed from what they had just witnessed.

During a break in the show, Rosemary chatted it up with the audience—as she was known to do. She moved on to introducing her conductor John Oddo and the members of the band. When she got to the drummer she said, "I'd like you folks to welcome my good friend John Signola," and John took a bow. Of course, the locals already knew it was pronounced "Von Ohlen" from his years in Indianapolis, but not another word was said. It was one of the best introductions he'd had. He went on to discover that Clooney had told Oddo she wanted John for the gig. From that day forward, John was her drummer. She had three regulars across the country: one for each coast, and Von Ohlen for the entire middle portion of the United States.

The drummer carries much of the load on his back in hitting marks when backing a performer. Deserved or not, it's not unusual for a singer to blame or give an angry look toward the person seated behind the drums when the music is off. Rosemary never did this. On stage she was top-notch. Von Ohlen smiles and says, "Man, she was a true professional and always great to work with." John accompanied Rosie on all her shows as part of her smaller trio and when she performed with the Cincinnati Pops Orchestra. Another local talent who was a frequent performer with her band was bassist Michael Sharfe. John and Michael have played together for years in the Blue Wisp Big Band and the Steve Schmidt Trio.

Her musical director was John Oddo, who has worked with such names as Woody Herman, Michael Feinstein, and

Johnny Mercer. The arranger behind her music was the talented Johnny Mandel. Mandel studied at the Manhattan School of Music and Julliard. He's worked with a who's who of talent. Just two of his more recognizable compositions are "The Shadow of Your Smile" and the theme from *M*A*S*H*, "Suicide is Painless."

Rosemary's phrasing was flawless, her voice warm, smooth, and relaxed. She was sensitive and one hundred percent emotionally connected to a ballad as she transported the audience with her voice. The memories of performing with Rosemary are still rich in John's heart. Sitting behind his drums as Rosie sang was a magical experience. On numerous occasions he was brought to tears as she sang one of her classic ballads. He wondered more than once how Rosie seemed to stay so composed. "It was just beautiful," he says now.

John worked with Rosemary Clooney for twenty-some years, whether it was a trio, seven-piece band, or as part of a full symphony. They covered much of the United States and played all sorts of venues, including, of course, Cincinnati. When she performed with the Cincinnati Pops Orchestra and conductor Erich Kunzel, John was on the drums.

Kunzel was a showman through and through, and he knew how to throw a party. There was a Fourth of July event with the Pops back in 2000 that included Rosemary, host Nick Clooney, trumpeter Doc Severinsen, the United States Army Field Band and Soldiers' Chorus, the Southern Gateway Chorus, country fiddler Billy Contreras, the Camp Chase Fifes and Drums, the Cincinnati Gymnastics Academy, the University of Cincinnati College-Conservatory of Music Musical Theatre department, and a full volley of fireworks. The show was broadcast on PBS.

Clooney and the Cincinnati Pops shared billing another night with Buddy Rich. Of course, Buddy didn't play backup to anyone. The evening began with Rich playing with his own band, backed up by the Pops. Then Rosemary took the stage with John on drums along with the Pops. Buddy's band joined in, but nobody played Buddy's drum set, so John brought his own. John remembers Rich was loads of fun. The famous drummer was just one of the gang, joking and talking it up backstage with Rosie and the other musicians.

John remembers one Sunday morning after playing with Rosemary and the Pops the night before. It was a lazy sunny day and he was walking his dog not far from his home in Covington, a small community across the river from Cincinnati. Along rolled Erich Kunzel in his convertible. When the conductor recognized John he slowed down, and with a smile yelled, "I hate drummers!" John almost hollered, "Drummers hate conductors!" but out of respect he just gave a laugh and kept walking.

One of the last gigs John played with Rosemary was late 2001 in Houston, Texas. It was an afternoon banquet celebration for a large and very successful company that had something to do with the oil business. From the fine wine to the fancy suits, the event dripped with money. As dinner plates were cleared and glasses topped off, Rosemary and her band kicked it into high gear. As part of the show she always enjoyed a bit of friendly banter with her audience. She'd entertain the crowd with stories involving friends like Bing Crosby and Frank Sinatra. The audience usually loved hearing about some of the biggest names from the golden age of Hollywood.

The unusual thing about this gig was most in attendance just sat on their hands, apparently uninterested or unfamiliar with many of those famous names. Rosie reminisced about the magical days working with the likes of Doris Day and Bob Hope, but as she looked out at the audience all she saw were blank stares. More than once she gave a look back at John and the other musicians, followed by a smile and shrug as the young crowd sat in relative silence. The employees were generally young; many in upper management were not far removed from college. They were all on a fast track to success with a company called Enron. It wasn't long after that the news of the financially imploding company hit. America watched as employees left the building in shock, as the doors were closed on Enron, which had seemed only weeks before to be one of the most successful companies in the country.

Rosemary Clooney was warm and friendly with John. They had deep a professional respect for what each contributed. Von Ohlen and Michael Sharfe miss her warmth, spirit, and the great charts they would play. John respected Rosie's privacy too. They'd played plenty of gigs together over the years but had their individual scars and stories. John knew he was in the presence of a special lady. Rosie had been through the glamorous highs of "White Christmas" and Bing Crosby to the really tough lows, much of it with the public having a front-row seat. She'd seen it all, but always maintained her friendly, local-girl attitude.

There was another time when they were just chatting it up and Rosemary told John she'd just returned from the Mayo Clinic in Rochester. "Well, they've taken it all away from me: no booze, no smoking, and no fun," she said. They both chuckled.

They'd still find a way to have a few drinks after a show, her holding court with a few of the guys, swapping stories and sharing a few laughs. She was always fun. He remembers one time when Rosemary told an interviewer, "I just don't give a damn. You just gotta be yourself and take it from there." She had been through so much and still had that special sparkle. It was a terribly sad day when she died.

Photo: Playing at Rosemary Clooney's sixtieth birthday party. Left to right: Lee Stoller, Mary Ellen, Lou **Louche** on bass, and John.

Music Is Family and Love

The songbook of John's life changed forever in the late 1980s when another special lady entered his world. No one can say it better than he does: "It was hook, line, and sinker. The trap door opens and you just go." John met Mary Ellen Tanner.

Mary Ellen was pretty, and "*man*, could she sing." But what made it work so well over the years for the two free-spirited artists was an accepting and unconditional love. They didn't try to change each other. Musically they got along too. John knew how to play behind a singer and they played together often over the years, including regular gigs in Cincinnati at the Celestial, Chez Nora (now "Lisse"), and the Blue Wisp Jazz Club.

Mary Ellen had a saying that was framed on the wall at home: "Friends are family we meet along the way." She had a warm and loving heart, and their dearest friends have been fellow musicians and folks who had come into their lives.

Photo: Accompanying Mary Ellen on a Bob Braun Promotional Cruise sometime in the 1990s.

Mary Ellen was another local talent. She started with Deke Moffitt when she was just twelve years old. She worked with top artists including Bob Hope, Liberace, Paul Williams, the Les Brown Orchestra, and an assortment of the area's best musicians. There's little doubt she could have made a name for herself in New York City and other big cities, but she was loyal to the area and to her friends. Mary Ellen was best known for the many years she appeared and sang on the *Bob Braun Show*, and with long-time accompanist Lee Stoller on piano. Cal Collins called her "a pearl—professional, consistent, and polished." Mary Ellen and John were together for almost thirty years, until her death in 2014.

Rosemary Clooney entertained numerous times in Cincinnati, including magical nights under the stars with the Cincinnati Pops. After the show, when John was back home with Mary Ellen, it wasn't unusual for the phone to ring and the two ladies would chat it up about everything from singing to what the local gang was up to. They'd been friends for years, and Rosemary was kind of like a mentor to Mary Ellen. She'd be performing somewhere and Ms. Clooney would grab a table with a few friends and spend the evening enjoying the lovely sounds as her friend sang.

Photo: Playing at Chez Nora, a venue in Covington that Mary Ellen and Lee Stoller played often, with John on drums.

Mary Ellen, Lee Stoller, John, and Lou Louche performed at the memorial for Rosemary in her hometown of Maysville, Kentucky. The event was attended by a large collection of longtime fans, celebrities, friends, and family. It's hard to describe one as separate from another. Rosie had so many fans and entertainers who'd worked with the kind and talented singer. Over time, John has grown to know the entire Clooney family and they couldn't be friendlier or more welcoming.

Musicians are John's clan. The hours spent with musicians, the countless hours behind the scenes, out on stage, or traveling all night to  the next gig creates a bond that is deeper than blood relatives. Music can be a language all its own, creating a feeling or buzz that words can't compete with. These were the people he understood, and who understood him. Duke Ellington said, "Music is my mistress." Music and musicians are John's family.

John grew up an only child who was comfortable and happier on his own. The concept of a family of brothers, sisters, and relatives was foreign and not an intuitive thing for him. Raised by his grandmother and a very loving father, he was still on his own much of the time.

Photo: Just messing around, probably at Chez Nora.

John developed a vivid imagination and could easily entertain himself as a kid. Little Johnny would strap on his six-gun, step out the back door, and wander in search of whatever varmint needed to be dealt with. The hours upon hours spent playing drums and toying with different sounds were a positive result of his independent and curious mind.

On the other hand, Mary Ellen was what would have to be called a "people person." She was popular and well known around town. She had a warm and easy way about her and for years was seen daily on the *Bob Braun Show*. As John and Mary Ellen spent more time together, he'd accompany her to fancy parties and social events. It wasn't unusual for a host or guest to go out of his way to have a chat with the new guy (John), but from investments to golf scores it was a language Von Ohlen didn't speak and had no interest in.

His life has been music and sitting behind a drum set. The workday for John ended long after the gig was over when the sun might not be far from coming up. John certainly knows hard work and dedication, but he wouldn't know a straight corporate job if it attacked him in a three-piece suit. Until he met Mary Ellen, his most important and intimate relationship outside of his father and music had been with Master. After a couple of years John and Mary Ellen agreed "no more" to the fancy parties. They came to an even deeper acceptance of what was important to them as a couple and individually.

Photo: Mary Ellen, John, and George Van Epps—one of John's all-time favorite musicians—in the early 1990s.

Chautauqua Music Festival

In the '80s, John started playing at the Chautauqua Music Festival in upstate New York. Today the Chautauqua Institution offers lectures, learning seminars, the performing arts, and various artistic entertainment. It pulls in a diverse collection of world-class experiences and speakers, including Ken Burns, Julie Andrews, and David McCullough. Concerts and musical offerings cover a spectrum of sound including contemporary jazz, classical, and rock 'n' roll. The learning center and institute has facilities over a wide geographic area, with much of it located on beautiful Chautauqua Lake in New York State.

John started participating in the Chautauqua Festival during the 1980s. A fellow named Joe Bouton organized a portion that focused on straight-ahead Dixieland jazz. For over thirty years John was asked to play, and in his usual expressive fashion says, "God, I loved it—*man* he'd hired the best of that bag." Bouton would hire the best to play Dixieland style, not "bebop." Some of the musicians John had never heard of, and there were other well-known artists like George Van Epps, Jimmy Rowles, Ralph Sutton, Joe Wilder, and Bobby Haggard. Many brought skills and memories from another era, like blues singer Maxine Sullivan, who started out in the speak-easies of Pittsburgh.

They'd usually play with four or seven musicians at different venues around the area or specifically at the festival. The musicians would occasionally offer short teaching clinics, but never the four-to-seven-week seminars offered elsewhere throughout the institute. As a kid, John had played and dug the heck out of Dixieland, and the chance to play with the various musicians Bouton brought in was super.

The whole experience was another example of John's continued desire to challenge himself artistically and play with the best, drawing some of the biggest names in jazz, with an emphasis on that more traditional sound. The music and musicians leaned toward what was played in the '20s, '30s, and '40s, with a heavy influence toward Dixieland, rather than contemporary or even big band. For John, the experience brought together rare and diverse performers in a celebration of "pure music." The atmosphere was slightly happier and carefree, rather than the more serious approach to jazz that sometimes is found in contemporary music circles.

After Joe Bouton passed away, his family continued for a couple more years in New York, but eventually the program was sold to someone with Northern Ohio roots. The whole shebang was moved to Cleveland and took up residency at a location not far from the Cleveland Clinic. The musicians and focus seemed to change and after all those years, John stopped attending around 2010.

When asked for any stories, Von Ohlen says of course there was the music, and then he chuckles. "Man, we would play at these majestic older hotels located along the lake for like a week at a time. As we were leaving this one famous place, all these great-looking chicks started showing up. Only later did we discover that a convention for cross-dressers was about to begin."

A Few Other Gigs

Even though John had decided he was done with life on the road, there were still some out-of-town shows that he wouldn't turn down. They include joining Cal Collins and the great Benny Goodman in an all-acoustic performance in Norfolk, Virginia. With no rehearsal, the drummer joined the band using mainly brushes for what was a terrific experience. To this day, John says Benny really was "the King of Swing."

In 1988, John was contacted to sub for drummer Jeff Hamilton on a two-week tour of Japan, backing Mel Tormé. Hamilton is one of the top drummers in the country, and a student and fan of John's. What excited Von Ohlen about the job was the chance to play with Marty Paich, the talented arranger and composer. The tour was top-notch, producing some great music.

In 1989, John traveled to Cologne, Germany, for a two-week gig with the internationally famous WDR Big Band,

as they backed Carmen McRae.

No disrespect to the singer who was a wonderful talent, but what really grabbed John's attention was the chance to play with the orchestra.

Making enough money to live is a necessary consideration for John, but new musical experiences and playing with the best is often worth more than money.

Photo: Location unknown.

The WDR Big Band evolved along with the entire WDR radio station after World War II. It has become an ambassador of music around the globe, drawing a who's who of talent. This particular opportunity included the chance for John to play with John Clayton, the masterful composer, arranger, and bass player. When the call came, the drummer was all in. The band rehearsed for a week on their own, and then Carmen flew in for a second week and more rehearsals. Much of the music over those two weeks was recorded, but there were never plans to have anything distributed for sale. That changed ten years later when Quincy Jones heard the tapes. He acquired the rights and *Dream of Life* was produced and released.

In the 1980s, both John and Mary Ellen started teaching at the University of Cincinnati College-Conservatory of Music. Considered one of the premier music schools in the country, CCM's director of jazz studies, Rick VanMatre, hired John as an adjunct instructor.

Von Ohlen seems to be able to pull the positive from almost any experience, and this has been the case in working with younger drummers. John enjoys the different students, and they keep him abreast of some of the hottest or newest trends in music. He focuses less on technique and more on feel, broadening awareness and encouraging students to find their own unique style. Von Ohlen is not a tactician and doesn't believe dogma has any place in jazz.

John believes there is some wonderful young talent around, but there is too much attention on playing the fast, complicated beats of rock 'n' roll, and on playing loud. After all the years of exploring different sounds and nuances, John is a master at introducing these ingredients into how he plays the drums. He works at changing up the tempo and pulling an unlimited collection of sounds off the drums and cymbals. He stays away from lectures and formal classes, opening different paths in getting to the desired goal.

John's spiritual awareness affects every part of his life. Part of his self-understanding is that we all have different "parts," or aspects of ourselves. For him there are "two selves." There is the "me" who is fun-loving, and there is the "me" who is closer to his inner life. When he meditates or gets more in touch with his inner world, it is a quieter, private place. Of course, anyone who has tried to verbalize such a personal journey also knows that words are limiting in this discussion. But his goals have become more "inner" at this stage in his life, and they affect everything, including his work with students.

Long Ago and Far Away

When John agreed he wanted to take part in this small book, he was adamant that the story should include more than just his musical career. Meeting Ed Zimmerman and Master changed his life. John will tell you it saved his life. John is sometimes reluctant to go into detail about his deeper beliefs and Master. He explains that he doesn't talk about it because "some folks think it is some kind of cult, or they just don't get it and it is hard to explain." He says, "It is kind of like musicians, you can have passable ones and then destructive ones, and every now and then you get a really great one! Like Louis Armstrong or Charlie Parker—and that is the same with Master—he is one of the rare and truly special ones."

In our physical form we are ruled by desire. And we will continue to do what we do because of this. When we die, we leave this physical body but are still left with desire, including pure emotion and intellect. There will come a time when an individual no longer wants to be ruled by their desires. This will take numerous lifetimes, but it is a journey toward self-realization, meaning you no longer want to be pulled into this world of cravings and desires. But we don't just decide we're ready.

Belief systems are such a personal thing, and trying to describe someone else's journey is even more limiting. Many things have influenced who John is today, but none more than Hinduism and especially Master. The Self is God, and all souls become stronger through experiences and lifetimes to become Self. God is in everyone, and Master helped John on his own journey with Self. John was disciplined and did his best to turn himself over to the teachings of the practice.

But as John says, he wasn't ready for a life of total devotion. He wasn't ready to leave this world behind. He wasn't ready to give up music and other desires. But his travels and experiences changed him, as life can for us all, especially if we have any degree of self-awareness and are attempting to live a more conscious life.

Master, Mary Ellen, his father, and Stan Kenton were special in their own ways for John. Each had a tremendous impact on his life. And then there are the many friends he's made and musicians he's met around the country, in Cincinnati, and at the Blue Wisp. He would not be who he is without these experiences that color every part of his life.

In reflecting on life, John often brings up Ralph Waldo Emerson. Emerson said, "Do what you do naturally and you'll create a need for it." Because of this, he has helped start numerous Big Bands, reaching out and pulling the best musicians together. The same could be said for other musical efforts. There may not initially appear to be a vocal demand for Big Bands, but John has followed his instincts. There is a theme in his life that can be seen in how he plays his drums, works with students, and attempts to live life. He plays how he feels. You must do what you do; it's not healthy to disregard or deny the pull in your life. But he also believes that deep changes don't happen through simple force of will. Your spirit must be ready.

John tried Christianity and was even baptized twice. It just wasn't for him, and when he met Master and began his journey, it worked. In future lifetimes he will continue to travel in that direction. But who better than John himself to describe the path of his current life? "For now, it's good old 4/4, bebop, and jazz."

Good Music

I have known John from a distance for over thirty years. Anyone living in the Cincinnati area with at least a passing interest in jazz and the drums would be hard-pressed not to be familiar with who he is. I also lived across the street from John and Mary Ellen in Covington, Kentucky, for about eight years. Occasionally we'd say hello on the street, or I'd confirm the Big Band was playing that Wednesday night, which of course they were. It wasn't unusual to walk past whatever old car John was driving at the time, parked on the street with an entire drum set loaded onto the passenger seats.

Around the end of 2014, we started chatting a bit and I asked him if he'd ever thought of doing a book about his life. Sadly, Mary Ellen had passed away and maybe he had a bit more time on his hands, but he was interested. "Nothing fancy," John said, "maybe just a collection of pages bound together telling a bit of my story." The idea started to get legs, and I approached a publisher and a professional writer. There was interest, but the idea didn't come together. I told John, "I'm not a professional, but heck, I'll write it." Of course, since having learned how laid-back John can be, it's no surprise he would say, "sure."

The story told here is the result of many hours spent talking over coffee at the Roebling Point Books & Coffee shop in Covington. John also kept a cassette deck at home and talked about whatever memories hit him at that moment. I prodded him with questions and requests for stories, and he did his best. No doubt there is more left out from his life than is included in these pages, but hopefully we hit a few of the more interesting and life-changing events. I am drawn to free spirits, so getting to know John has been an extra treat. As a bit of a searcher and drummer myself, I've especially enjoyed our conversations about music, the drums, and his spiritual journey. It's been a treat entering John's world a bit, and I hope you enjoyed it too.

In memory of our friend, John Von Ohlen.

May 13, 1941 – October 3, 2018

Photo: Book signing, February 2017.